To those who have suffered much but believed even more

that there is a God who not only loves us unconditionally,

but likes us so completely

His heart smiles every time He thinks of us

—and He thinks of us constantly.

The Rock of Roseville
725 Vernon St., Roseville, CA
95678 U.S.A.

www.rockofroseville.org
www.rockspots.tv

Cover design by Hans Bennewitz

ISBN:
13-: 978-0-9824967-6-3

LIVING PERFECTLY POSITIONED

NO. 1

daily enjoying the only life you have

"LOVING LIFE" DEVOTIONAL SERIES

FRANCIS ANFUSO

ACKNOWLEDGMENT

In *Perfectly Positioned*, I acknowledged the many people who have contributed to my life and this project. I am eternally grateful to each for their love and care for me, which in turn has made possible this book.

Even though some have not been directly involved in this present devotional, I am compelled to at least mention them by name, and in the original order. Without the help of each of these wonderful people, there would be no book.

My dear mother, brothers and sisters: Victor, Joseph, Diana and Maria; my beautiful wife Suzie and our amazing children, Deborah and Havilah; the great Rock Interns, my pastoral assistant Lydia Birks, and the principal editor of *Perfectly Positioned*, Natalie Eiferd.

Each were a lifeline to me.

Helping in this particular volume has once again been Hans Bennewitz, our gifted graphic artist and layout aficionado, and the easiest man in the world to get along with.

The principal architect of the project and my creative assistant is Stephanie VanTassell. She has done a magnificent job in guiding all aspects of the book, and was the one who "made it happen."

Further editing was provided and much appreciated by Tamara Johnston, Betty Price and Dr. Kandee Mamula.

To all, my deepest appreciation and thanks.

Lives will be changed because of you.

Francis Anfuso
Thanksgiving 2009

INTRODUCTION

When I say "If God could do it for me, He could do it for anyone," it's because I was so messed up that God straightening out my heart and mind was nothing short of a miracle. A former suicidal atheist, being neurotic was all I knew.

But God, in His mercy, rescued my life, and gave me the grace and insight to rescue others. Before writing the book, *Perfectly Positioned*, and after decades of watching God transform my own life, He spoke to my heart, "I've given you the cure for cancer of the soul!"

The many people who have since read *Perfectly Positioned* affirmed this conviction.

Now, the first in a three-part *"Loving Life" Devotional Series, Living Perfectly Positioned*, breaks the hundreds of life-transforming revelations into 122 days of devotions. They are sequenced in such a way that the journey to spiritual wholeness will be both gradual and thorough.

You will be able to chew on these nuggets throughout your day, and take them with you for the rest of your life. My life has been so healed, I'm absolutely filled with faith that God can do the same for you.

Today, make the commitment to devour this book. Begin the journey. In 1/3 of a year, you can see your entire perspective of life, past, present and future revolutionized.

As God has no favorites, if He healed me, He can heal you.

Francis Anfuso

122 Days—Living Perfectly Positioned

DAY 01 Set Up To Fail

PRINCIPLE: IT'S IMPOSSIBLE FOR A BLAMELESS GOD TO DO ANYTHING BUT GOOD.

Have you ever felt like God set you up to fail?

The greatest miracles I've ever seen took place in media projects that God never intended me to complete. Try filing that one away.

It would take me years to fully process what had gone on and come to terms with God's ultimate intention for each life-altering situation. Even though today I am completely at peace with the death of those projects, in the past it was not always so. It seemed not only out of character for God to allow such mixed messages, but emotionally criminal. I was convinced my appeal to a higher court in Heaven would certainly receive a different verdict. But, for what seemed an eternity, my petitions were unanswered.

I have come to believe that "onward and upward" is in fact a non-Biblical perspective. Though somewhat overstated, "onward and downward" would be much closer to the truth. "Before honor is humility." (Proverbs 18:12) God always defaults to what is ultimately in our best interest and therefore has no intention of fulfilling all of our dreams.

As the One who shaped and fashioned our inner needs, why would God fulfill a dream He knows is inherently unfulfilling? It's taken me half a lifetime to realize that His commitment is to fulfill His dream for me, which is infinitely better, though inevitably hidden from my eyes.

"It is God's privilege to conceal things and the king's privilege to discover them." (Proverbs 25:2, NLT) God's motive in this high-stakes game of hide-and-seek is pure and purposeful, though our experience on earth can be, at times, extremely painful. Many who have gone through unexplainable tragedy, often arriving at a life-altering crossroad with a broken heart, have come to a far different conclusion about the motive of God. One songwriter summed up human existence with this rather bleak assessment, "Life sucks, and then you die." How heartwarming!

Though this statement may contain a small measure of truth, it by no means accurately portrays what life's about. God is not some cosmic killjoy getting His jollies out of pulling the wings off of helpless humans. In fact, quite the opposite is true. It is impossible for a blameless God to do anything but good.

"And we know that all things work together for good to those who love God, to those who are the called according to His purpose." (Romans 8:28)

1. **What have been the greatest letdowns in your life?**

2. **Have you seen God working in them, using each painful experience for your good?**

   If not, look again, asking God to reveal His marvelous plan and purpose for the lowest moments in your life.

DAY 02 Peeling My Heart Off Closed Doors

PRINCIPLE: MY UNDERSTANDING OF ALL I HAVE BEEN THROUGH HAS ECLIPSED THE LONGING FOR WHAT I MAY HAVE MISSED.

How do you survive hitting a brick wall?

Once, while visiting with friends, I watched a seven-year-old boy run in and out of the house all afternoon. As the day wore on and the temperature dropped, the boy's mother decided to close the sliding glass door leading into the back yard. Somehow the little guy didn't notice, and a few moments later, going 50 mph, he smashed into the invisible barrier. He didn't just fall backward—he was propelled backward. He hit the glass so hard, I thought, "He's dead! There's no way he could have survived that!"

But much to our amazement, a few minutes later, after readjusting his nose, he was up and about, though moving a little slower.

I once had media projects that died a slow death, and I felt exactly like that battered boy. I hit a brick wall with the "pedal to the metal." The wind didn't just leave my sails; God forcibly removed it. My heart sank in disbelief as I tried to grasp the unexpected turn of events. I was completely at a loss. Why had God consistently shown His hand of favor in each venture? Why would He allow me to invest so much time and energy on each of these worthwhile projects if He didn't want them completed? Why would He have me pray and see my prayers answered, only to ultimately watch each endeavor melt into oblivion? Frankly, it seemed unspeakably cruel.

With each of these projects I stood waiting, as a faithful sentry, by open doors of opportunity only to have them abruptly slammed in my face. Yet, I refused to believe these shut doors would remain closed forever. The remarkable miracles I had seen God perform seemed to refute that possibility. So I continued to stand outside the doors and wait for them to reopen. The waiting turned into years.

In the end, I would accept the inevitable: these endeavors were on life support and I would have to pull the plug. I had to let my dreams die, walking away both shaking my head and shaken to the core.

Presently, if these opportunities suddenly materialized and I could be guaranteed their success, yet lose all that I had learned in the struggle, I'd say, "Thanks, but no thanks." The hard-fought revelations are far more significant and meaningful to me than seeing any of the projects completed.

Ask God to reveal the true value of your pain. Though not all will be shown to you at this time, more than enough will be revealed to make every ounce of pain worth it.

"Don't be surprised at the fiery trials you are going through. Instead, be very glad—for these trials make you partners with Christ in his suffering, so that you will have the wonderful joy of seeing his glory when it is revealed to all the world." (1Peter 4:12–13, NLT)

1 **Has your understanding of all you have been through eclipsed the longing for what you missed?**

2 **Have you gone past the point of regret and savored the transforming revelation of God's purpose in your struggles?**

DAY

03 Irreversible Horror

PRINCIPLE: THE GREATEST LESSONS IN LIFE ARE PRIMARILY THE RESULT OF LEARNING TO RESPOND PROPERLY TO WHAT WE PERCEIVE AS FAILURE OR LOSS.

How do you resolve things you wish never happened?

When I was about ten years old, one of my great adventures in life was catching large bullfrogs. I loved the thrill of sneaking up behind them and then, moving at light speed, plucking them out of the water with one fell swoop. Their skin felt so funny; it was rubbery and slippery, covered with strange bumps. But, however long the hunt took, my exploits with bullfrogs always came down to catch and release—except on one tragic occasion.

One day, I caught a really big bullfrog. I had the bizarre thought that it would be fun to peel off his skin and see what was underneath. Everything seemed to go fine until I dropped the skinless frog back onto the hot sand. Only then did I fully realize the tragic mistake I had made. In horror I stared at the hapless victim now shrouded in sand.

His life was soon over.

What started out as a neat idea turned into an ordeal I desperately wanted to reverse. Incapable of devising a plan to get his skin back on, I could only watch the doomed frog writhe in pain. Finally, unable to bear it any longer, I walked away feeling terribly sick inside. Forty-five years later I'm still embarrassed over what I did to that poor little frog.

Life is full of situations we wish never happened. Many of them are self-inflicted, while others are part of the script we have been given. Only with God's help can we properly respond to them, living—and eventually dying—in peace. Fortunately, God seems to take special pleasure in showing His power in our mistakes and weakness—even in the unspeakable experiences we go through.

The greatest lessons in life are primarily the result of learning to respond properly to what we perceive as failure or loss. Looking back now, I wouldn't change a thing, even though my perceived failure was so devastating at the time. I see now that God is able to use even failure for my good as I continue to trust Him.

Have you seen that in your own life?

Has what you've gained outweighed what you've lost?

Ask God to show you the true scales of Heaven.

None of us have been cheated. And none of our regrets are worth dwelling on once they've been covered by the gracious love and blood of Jesus.

"Love covers all sins." (Proverbs 10:12)

1. **When you look at your failures and regrets through the lens of Proverbs 10:12, what is the Lord revealing to you?**

2. **Has what you've gained outweighed what you've lost?**

DAY 04

Lousy Timing, Perfect Moment

PRINCIPLE: THE SITUATIONS YOU LEAST EXPECT OR DESIRE TO HAPPEN CAN BECOME DECISIVE MOMENTS FOR YOUR GOOD, IF YOU RESPOND WELL.

How do you survive life's setbacks?

When my wife, Suzie, and I had been married for just nine months, I went to Montreal, Quebec to film during the 1976 Olympics. A small film crew and I traveled from California to film Christians publicly sharing their faith outside Olympic venues.

The day before the Olympics began, I called home to hear that a doctor had told Suzie, who was three months pregnant, she was probably having a miscarriage. The news was jarring. We prayed and I offered to take the next plane back to California, but she insisted I stay. My courageous wife, knowing how important the filming was to me, was resolute that I did not need to return home and that she would be fine.

Hanging up the phone, I prayed with the other members of our film crew for God's direction. After much prayer and discussion, it was obvious to everyone that my priority was to catch the next plane home to be with my wife.

On the day the Olympics started and filming began, after months of grueling preparation, I found myself boarding a plane—doing the right thing—but hating every minute of it. I was mad. I loved my wife and wanted to be there for her, but why did God have to pick one of the most important events in my young Christian life to ask for my obedience? His timing seemed, to say the least, really lousy!

Suzie had gone to stay with her parents for emotional support. I decided not to call, but to surprise her. When I arrived at her folks' home, she was totally shocked to see me standing there with flowers. Bursting into tears, we hugged and cried. It was a very moving moment. Even her dad, an atheist who rarely showed emotion, choked up when he greeted me and, looking into my eyes, said, "Son, you did the right thing!"

I have no doubt that, when Dad finally gave his heart to Jesus many years later, some of the first seeds of trust were sown on that fateful day. As her father, he didn't care if a video was made or not. But what he did care about was that his daughter's husband was willing to give up even the most important thing he was doing to come to her aid. People will see far more of God in us by how we respond to failure than to success.

Suzie had the miscarriage. It was a sad and painful loss, but a gigantic statement had been made. A pillar was put in place that remains steadfast throughout over 30 years of marriage. Wherever I am in the world, whatever work I am doing, if Suzie needs me, I will drop everything else and come to her side. One year later, God graciously gave us two beautiful, identical twin daughters. For God so loved...He gave.

Would you pray today for God to prepare your heart for the disappointments ahead? The situations you least expect or desire to happen can become decisive moments for your good, if you respond well.

It was the will of God to "...test them in the wilderness to see what was in their hearts."

1. **How has God turned a disappointment in your life into a decisive moment?**

2. **How do you think your responses to disappointments have affected you/others?**

DAY

05 The Road To Hope

PRINCIPLE: CHARACTER IS ONLY DEVELOPED THROUGH STRUGGLES.

How do you develop character?

The words of the Apostle Paul have helped me on many occasions during my times of setback and failure. “We rejoice in our sufferings,” he writes, “because we know that suffering produces perseverance; perseverance, character; and character, hope.” (Romans 5:3–4, NIV)

Working this spiritual equation backwards we find that if we lack hope, it is because we lack character; if we lack character, it is because we lack perseverance; and if we lack perseverance, it is because we have not responded properly to the trials and tribulations that face us. You don’t get character by sitting in a hot tub eating ice cream. Character is only developed through struggles. Shakings are essential to life. We must go through them in order to experience “the removal of those things that are being shaken, as of things that are made, that the things which cannot be shaken may remain.” (Hebrews 12:27)

Jim Elliot rightly said, “God always gives His best to those who leave the choice with Him.” If we remain steadfast, confidently embracing God’s providential plan, the final chapter of our lives will reveal His infinite wisdom and matchless destiny. Only He can take a shattered dream and multiply its potential a hundredfold.

In some dimension of your life, you need God’s character to be formed in you.

1 Do you lack hope? Are you discouraged about situations in your life? Has what you’ve gained outweighed what you’ve lost?

DAY 06 In Case of Failure, Read This!

PRINCIPLE: UNTIL I AM DESPERATE TO FULLY EMBRACE MY CONVICTIONS, I WILL NEVER CHANGE.

How do you get God to move… to answer your prayers?

Failure is an inevitable part of life, but we still have a choice as to how we will respond. We can choose to hide our failures and weaknesses from others out of embarrassment and fear, or we can choose to view these times as opportunities to see the areas in our lives that still need work. Embarrassment alone isn't enough to drive us to change. It is not until we get truly desperate that we will be sufficiently motivated to pursue changing our lives.

Embarrassment is merely the first stage of conviction. When we see areas in our lives that are out of control, we feel embarrassed. However, that is only the beginning of the sufficient provocation needed for change. Embarrassment is a junior stage of conviction—actually, a baby step. People live and die embarrassed but never really change. Expressions such as, "I know I shouldn't do it, but I do!" or, "It's a horrible habit" merely gloss over an underlying lack of dedication to change. In Luke 9:45, the disciples "were embarrassed to ask him [Jesus] what He meant." (The Message) Embarrassment brought about no eternal change. They were not yet ready.

The next stage of conviction is being fed up. When we are fed up, we no longer try to hide our failures; we attempt to fix them ourselves. Here again, though a person may be sick and tired of acting a certain way, being fed up will only produce depression or anger and not a lasting change in behavior.

A disciple is a whole-hearted follower of Jesus Christ. Jesus affirmed this when He challenged, "So likewise, whoever of you does not forsake all that he has cannot be My disciple." (Luke 14:33) Partial commitments produce insufficient results.

What is needed is a departure from conventional wisdom. We can live and die both embarrassed and fed up and still see no tangible alteration of our behavior. Until we see our departure from sin as a life-and-death issue, requiring a desperate response, we will never rise to the level of concern that facilitates personal transformation. It isn't until we reach the final stage of conviction—desperation—that we will see the change we truly desire in our lives. We have to be desperate for God in order to be yielded to Him.

The psalmist cried out, "I'm in trouble. I cry to God, desperate for an answer…" (Psalm 120:1, The Message) Will you pause right now and cry out to God?

What has God convicted you about? Will you respond to His Spirit and make a desperate appeal for Him to break off specific areas of bondage in your life?

"The effective, fervent prayer of a righteous man avails much." (James 5:16)

1. **What is God currently convicting you about?**
2. **What stage of conviction are you experiencing: a) embarrassment, b) being fed up, or c) desperation?**
3. **Look through Psalm 120:1. Experience the desperation of the psalmist and make your own appeal to God for Him to break off specific areas of bondage in your life.**

DAY 07

Breaking the Cycle of Deception

PRINCIPLE: WITHOUT EMBRACING GOD'S PERSPECTIVE, WE WILL EVENTUALLY FALL INTO DECEPTION.

What would you rather God change: your circumstances or your perspective?

Without embracing God's perspective, we will eventually fall into deception. God's not trying to change our circumstances; He's trying to change our reaction to them.

If the only way we learn is by making mistakes, instead of being dedicated to change, then we are destined to become an ugly mass of scar tissue. The Word and the Spirit of God purpose to guide us into truth and to spare us the heartbreaking anguish of serious failure. If we only learn by being enrolled in the School of Hard Knocks, then we will experience the way of the unfaithful, which is unnecessarily hard. (Proverbs 13:15)

How does this cycle of deception take place? Sin first begins in our thoughts, then thoughts become deeds, deeds become habits, habits form our personality, and ultimately, our personality shapes our destiny. In a similar way, if we don't stop evil desires in the thought stage, eventually they will manifest themselves as deeds, which sooner or later become habits, gradually overtaking our personality until, in the end, they establish our destiny. "Then the evil desire, when it has conceived, gives birth to sin, and sin, when it is fully matured, brings forth death." (James 1:15, Amplified)

With God's power, we can stop thoughts before they become deeds, and deeds before they develop into habits. By breaking this cycle, we will live life flourishing in the oasis of God's personality and destiny.

"Therefore if the Son makes you free, you shall be free indeed." (John 8:36)

1 **Do you battle with deceptive thoughts? If so, pray for truth to set you free.**

DAY 08

The Cure is in the Disease

PRINCIPLE: FAILURE MUST BE REALIZED BEFORE SUCCESS CAN BE APPRECIATED.

How should you view the lowest moments in your life? My aged mother often said, "Before you can appreciate the good, you have to experience the bad." Though perhaps imperfect in her theology, this wise lady had tasted enough of life to know something of its sequencing. Just as pride comes before destruction, and humility before honor, so, too, we must know we are lost before we can be eternally saved. In a sense, the cure and the disease are inexorably linked.

Here is a perfect analogy elaborating on this profound principle. In order to provide protection and immunization from certain diseases, vaccines are developed which contain weakened or dead microbes of the kind that actually cause the disease in the first place. These inoculations stimulate the immune system to produce antibodies, which in turn fight the disease.

Jesus became sin for us in order "that we might become the righteousness of God in Him." (2Corinthians 5:21) He chose failure in order to secure everlasting success for those He loves. He allowed all of mankind's bad to be fully credited to His account. Christ's lowest moment became the launching point for our highest.

We have all misjudged God and His purpose for us. We have all given up too quickly. Our rescue is at hand if we will but wait, hope and believe. Will you willingly embrace the inevitable challenges of life that are, in fact, divinely prepared appointments with destiny? Will you allow God to renew your mind and heal your misconceptions of all that has transpired thus far?

1 What life experiences have caused you to misjudge God's good intentions for you in every situation?

DAY

09 Tragedies Redeemed

PRINCIPLE: GOD REVEALS HIMSELF BEST IN AREAS OF OUR LIVES THAT HURT THE MOST.

Is there value in the worst tragedies of life?

A fishing fleet left a small harbor in Newfoundland and was caught in a terrible storm. When night came, the ships were scheduled to return home, yet none of them did.

All night long, the mothers, wives, and children of the fishermen walked the shores looking for some sign of their loved ones, praying tearfully that God would bring them back safely. Adding to their anxieties, one of the homes in the village caught fire in the middle of the night. Since all of the men were gone, it burned to the ground.

But as morning dawned, the entire fleet of ships sailed safely back into the harbor. All of the villagers rejoiced when they saw their men safely home, except the woman whose home had burned down. Approaching her husband with grief written across her face, she cried out, "We are ruined! Our home and everything we had were destroyed by fire." Her husband, however, just shook his head. "What are you saying? Thank God for the fire!" he exclaimed. "It was the light of our burning home that guided the whole fleet into port."

Yes, in this world we will have tribulation. But Jesus says, "Be of good cheer; I have overcome the world!" (John 16:33) He has overcome the disasters of life. He has overcome the sin that infected us. If we will but trust Him—and Him alone—we are destined to be overcomers as well.

Have you seen God in your tragedies?

1 **What areas of your life have caused you the deepest hurts? Ask God to reveal Himself to you in these deep hurts. As you look through the lens of John 16:33, ask the Lord to help you become an overcomer in the arenas of life that have hurt you the most.**

DAY 10 Healing The Hurts

PRINCIPLE: THE FASTEST WAY TO GET TO THE LIFE OF YOUR DREAMS IS TO OBEY GOD.

Will God ever allow you to help people you once hurt?

Six months before I received Jesus, I was hitchhiking in Honolulu, Hawaii. An accountant from New York City and his family picked me up. He had shoulder-length hair, dabbled in smoking pot and was a poster child for counter-culture wannabes. Always ready to convert people to whatever I was into, I had an intense half-hour conversation trying to persuade him to give up his materialistic ways and pursue a more down-to-earth lifestyle. It was a sincere and meaningful conversation that, frankly, had no eternal value.

A year and a half later, after becoming a Christian, I was driving in New York City. As I was about to enter the busy Long Island Expressway, I saw a hitchhiker on the side of the onramp, whom I decided to pick up. As he got into the car, I instantly recognized him. He was the same accountant who had picked me up a year and a half before in Honolulu. We were both stunned. God's presence filled the vehicle, and I was suddenly aware of the fact that Jesus had fully orchestrated this divine appointment.

The man had unfortunately taken some of my misguided advice and had become a card-carrying member of the hippie subculture. For the next half-hour, talking at New York warp speed, I shared with this now-captive audience my complete testimony of God transforming my life as well as an impassioned overview of the gospel of Jesus Christ. The electricity in the car was palpable. We both knew our impossible rendezvous was sovereign.

Though at that moment he did not surrender his heart to Jesus, our lives were both shaken by the magnificent and flawless plan of God. This was one of the few times in my life I was able to impact the life of someone I had previously damaged. I treasure it as a moment when God once again redeemed the unredeemable, allowing failure to be eclipsed by faith.

Over the years, I have now had countless opportunities to help thousands of people who have made many of the same mistakes I once made. There is not a sin I have committed that I have not had the opportunity to tell another person about. There is not a type of person I have deceived whom I have not had the privilege of guiding into a saving relationship with the loving God of the Universe. There is not only life after failure, there is a redemptive purpose in every sin, every setback, and every heartbreak, we have or will ever go through.

The life of your dreams is just around the bend, and the fastest way to get there is obeying the will of God no matter how unfulfilling it may seem during the process.

Ask God to show you someone you can reach out to and help heal.

1. **In what ways is God redeeming your sins, setbacks and heartaches? Ask God to show you someone you can reach out to help from a place of healing in your own life.**

2. **As you look through the lens of Hebrews 5:8–9, what do you learn about the critical importance of obedience to God?**

DAY 11

Insignificant From Birth

PRINCIPLE: GOD REVEALS YOUR PERSONAL UNIQUENESS THROUGH THE PAIN IN YOUR LIFE.

How do you discover your personal significance?

My twin brother, Joseph, and I were born at the height of our father's political career. He was in his mid-40s and poised to be elected to five terms in the U.S. Congress. Having twin boys late in life was not a pleasant surprise. Consequently, neither was his response to us. My natural insecurities were soon fed by unnatural abandonment. In time, a supernatural God would heal both.

During the school year we lived in oppressively strict boarding schools from 11 years old on. We never lived at home again. It left me with deep feelings of personal inadequacy, anger toward my father and absolutely no idea who I was. What was it about me that my father disliked so much? Rejection and abandonment consumed my thoughts.

Each of us is born with an abiding sense of our own personal insignificance. We are herded like cattle through school lunch queues, grocery lines and traffic jams. Being ignored by our classmates, parents, and those closest to us frustrates our quest for self-importance. Yet, beneath the surface is an enduring hope that we do have some value, even if it is not yet revealed.

Ironically, because I grew up not living at home, it prepared me for two decades of globetrotting the world ministering to others. Because I was basically fatherless, I've had a passion to serve as a father to countless sons and daughters.

What have you been through in your youth that God will use as an adult? Ask God to reveal your personal uniqueness, the true value of all you have been through.

1 **How is God using your pain to fuel passion and purpose in your life?**

DAY 12 When You Hate Your Life

PRINCIPLE: : IT'S AMAZING WHAT WE CAN ENDURE FOR THE SAKE OF A LOVING TOUCH.

When I was a young boy in boarding school, I lived for years in a large room with 75 other boys—row after row of beds and dressers. I can hardly think of anything more impersonal and depressing. During my six years in this oppressively authoritative institution, we were never allowed to talk with our classmates—in any dorm room, classroom, hallway, bathroom, or shower. It was the loneliest experience of my life. I hated every minute of it. Even now, I cannot dwell on its emptiness without feeling heart sick.

There were no "good mornings," no "good nights," just whistles and threats. The priest in charge of our dorm wore a long black robe with a cross, but would drink beer, smoke cigars, and curse at us. He reminded me more of Judas than Jesus. It was like having a prisoner in charge of a prison. Since the day I graduated, I have never seen one person I went to grammar school or high school with. The year I left, they closed the boarding portion of the school down. Frankly, now 40 years later, it is still extremely painful to even think about.

During those forsaken years, I was so desperate for love and affection that I would periodically get up before the other boys and go to an early mass conducted in Latin, a language I didn't even understand. I would sit in those services, tired and bored to death, while all the other boys were sleeping, for just one reason.

In order to be awakened for the early mass, I had to tie a towel at the end of my bed the night before. The priest, seeing I wantod to go to the early mass and not wanting to make any noise to wake the other boys, would shake me for a few seconds. It was those precious moments of touch, even at the hand of someone I detested, that made it all worth it. I had been touched. Not in anger or correction, but I imagined, because someone cared.

It is embarrassing to write, but true just the same.

Will you let God touch your broken heart today?

He longs to fill your loneliness with His loving embrace.

1. Were there times in your life where you received a touch from someone who did not have your best interest in mind?
2. In what ways has the loving touch of Jesus impacted you?
3. In what areas do you still need to be touched?

DAY 13 Growing Up Fragile

PRINCIPLE: GOD'S SCRIPT IS DESIGNED TO HEAL MY PAST, ESTABLISH MY PRESENT, AND INSPIRE ME TO RUN TOWARD A FUTURE BEYOND MY WILDEST DREAMS.

Can God heal the injustice of your childhood?

God always gives His best to those who leave the choice with Him. Yet children, in truth, have few choices. For better or worse, other people direct most of their lives.

When I traveled as an itinerant evangelist I realized how much absolute control my wife Suzie and I had over our children. On a number of occasions we had to wake our pre-school age daughters, Deborah and Havilah, hours before first light, to begin a long journey across the country. We were always struck by how compliant our children were to our instructions.

"Get dressed girls, we have to leave soon!" Like toy soldiers they would obey our requests without question, seemingly walking in their sleep. Were they confident we knew what we were doing? No, I think they were merely following instructions.

For a season in my childhood I submissively ate the meals life dished out. But eventually, a closer examination of the food caused my frustration to boil over. When it did, no one was spared, least of all myself. I blamed everyone for my misery. Yet in the end, my loving Creator had written a foolproof script for me; it was designed to heal my past, establish my present, and inspire me to run toward a future beyond my wildest dreams. I am so thankful for the wonderful family I now have.

All of my brothers and sisters are following God. My wife and I have had decades of a marvelous relationship that only continues to get better. Our beautiful twin daughters married godly, caring men, and each daughter had their first child a week apart. I have a church family that consistently inspires me, as they lay down their lives for Jesus and one another. I am a truly blessed man!

Ask God to heal your past! Make the devil pay for all of the pain he has caused by using it to make you the person God always intended.

1. **Are you able to see God's blessings, even in the most challenging seasons of your life?**
2. **As you look through the lens of Jeremiah 29:11, what is revealed about God's heart for you?**

DAY 14 A Little Pain Goes A Long Way

PRINCIPLE: THE ULTIMATE BENEFIT OF BEING RESCUED AND HEALED IS THE EVENTUAL HONOR OF DOING THE SAME FOR OTHERS.

What is the real purpose of your pain?

Though it is impossible to fully relate and empathize with another person's pain, a little of our own pain goes a long way. My heart has broken countless times as battered people have shared the gruesome events of their deformed childhood.

Whether we like it or not, we will each have to look back long enough and deep enough to allow the Lord to heal us. If we refuse, then the abused will become the abuser, and the neglected will become the neglecter.

Our childhood may be so painful from abuse and neglect that we can spend years blocking it out. But we must still look back, through the healing eyes of a Creator who was with us during every horrific moment. He will take the years of turmoil and brokenness, and transform tortured memories into bridges of healing and hope; not only for ourselves, but also for those He will send our way.

As Paul the Apostle, once wrote, "So when we are weighed down with troubles, it is for your benefit and salvation! For when God comforts us, it is so that we, in turn, can be an encouragement to you."(2Corinthians 1:6a, NLT)

The ultimate benefit of being rescued and healed by Jesus is the honor of praising Him for His goodness, and the eventual privilege of doing the same for others. This is the paramount purpose of all we have been through.

May we not give up on our way to seeing its fulfillment.

1. **How have you been affected by God's healing power?**
2. **In what ways has your pain been redeemed by having opportunities to help heal others?**

DAY 15 Our Hurts Hide Our Hidden Worth

PRINCIPLE: CHARACTER ONLY COMES FROM RECEIVING THE LOVE OF GOD.

Our own hurts often keep us from seeing our hidden worth, which is not to be found in the high points of our life, but rather hidden under the rubble of our greatest pain. Only time, heat, and pressure can produce the most beautiful diamond. So too, as the Master Surgeon changes us. "Therefore if any man be in Christ, he is a new creature: old things are passed away; behold, all things are become new." (2Corinthians 5:17, KJV)

Though our struggles may at times seem pointless, the fruit of seeing life from God's perspective will last forever. The scales of Heaven, measuring everything in terms of eternity, will not miss an ounce of our true value. Though we think there is tragic waste in our lives, if we allow God to heal our hearts, the character being produced will far outweigh the pain suffered.

If you hear nothing else, hear this: character only comes from receiving the love of God. All attempts to change without first knowing how much God loves you will consign you to a life based on performance—what you can do—and not accepting what He has already done on your behalf. If we reject God's infinite love, we will try in vain to remake ourselves into the image of this fallen world, realizing only too late it was all for nothing. Receiving God's love will give us all the value we'll ever need.

Trade the sublime for the mediocre. Fight to see the beauty of God's love for you, rather than be crushed by the ashes of past disappointment.

1. **In what ways have you tried to gain God's love through performance?**

2. **As you look through the lens of Romans 8:35–39, what is most encouraging to you?**

DAY 16 Seduced By Life

PRINCIPLE: NOTHING OUTSIDE OF GOD'S PROMISES AND DESIRES FOR US WILL BRING THE SATISFACTION WE CRAVE.

Have you been seduced by life? All of us have!

A young boy in South Africa once swapped a costly diamond for a few toy soldiers. He was ignorant of what he had. Satan, the enemy of our soul, trifled away his own eternal value and now attempts to devalue as many other eternal beings as possible. Once known as Lucifer, the anointed worship leader of Heaven traded the priceless for the meaningless, when the love of God was all he would ever need.

In the end, there is no secret in our heart that our conduct will not reveal. In the beginning, charisma might get you going, but it will take character to keep you going. Though character may be seen in the great moments of our lives, it is formed in the small ones. The real limitations in our lives are only in us and in our character, never in the heart of a loving God. He will gladly fulfill our heart's desire once we fully embrace what is on His heart for us.

Though we are all seduced and distracted by the temporary pleasures of earth, "eternity is in our hearts," and nothing else will satisfy. (Ecclesiastes 3:11) Nothing outside of God's promises and desires for us will bring the satisfaction we crave.

My father had everything anyone could ask for—wealth, fame, family—yet without God what he sought after never fulfilled him. I refuse to pass on the lie. By God's grace, the curse has been broken.

Resolve to pass on the blessing of wealth that cannot be taken away—the eternal riches that cannot be seduced.

1 **As you look through the lens of John 10:10, what does abundant living look like to you?**

DAY 17 Blinded By Bitterness

PRINCIPLE: DON'T LET THE HEARTACHE CAUSED BY OTHERS DEFINE YOU. LET GOD TENDERIZE YOUR HEART.

Have you been blinded by bitterness?

The great philosopher Arthur Schopenhauer once said, "All truth passes through three stages. First, it is ridiculed. Second, it is violently opposed. Third, it is accepted as being self-evident." During my formative years I would mask the pain of being abandoned by my father with a casual indifference to his public distinction. But all of my vehement rejection of his disregard for my life only verified how important his approval really was.

The Bible says, "The glory of children is their fathers." (Proverbs 17:6, BBE) The original Hebrew language implies that this glory is "an ornament to be worn in honor… for all to behold its beauty." Even when bitterness blinded me from seeing the beauty of my father's glory, the longing for it was always there. It left me consigned to a lifelong tension: longing for his affection, while rejecting how insignificant thinking of him made me feel.

Young children are unable to differentiate between what is normal and healthy and what is merely common and dysfunctional. Without being able to understand that difference, my broken bond with my father led to an inherent distrust of all authority. I detested the duplicity between his public persona and our nonexistent private life.

Ask God to chip away the hardness in your heart. His promise is: "I will take away their hearts of stone and give them tender hearts instead…" (Ezekiel 11:19b, NLT)

Do it, Lord, tenderize my heart!

1 **How has the heartache caused by others defined you?**
In what ways have your responses affected your life/relationships?

DAY 18 Carried By Great Winds

PRINCIPLE: SELF-ABSORPTION KEEPS US FROM SEEING WHAT GOD IS DOING BEHIND THE SCENES IN EACH OF OUR LIVES.

Have you been seduced by life? All of us have!

A young boy in South Africa once swapped a costly diamond for a few toy soldiers. He was ignorant of what he had. Satan, the enemy of our soul, trifled away his own eternal value and now attempts to devalue as many other eternal beings as possible. Once known as Lucifer, the anointed worship leader of Heaven traded the priceless for the meaningless, when the love of God was all he would ever need.

In the end, there is no secret in our heart that our conduct will not reveal. In the beginning, charisma might get you going, but it will take character to keep you going. Though character may be seen in the great moments of our lives, it is formed in the small ones. The real limitations in our lives are only in us and in our character, never in the heart of a loving God. He will gladly fulfill our heart's desire once we fully embrace what is on His heart for us.

Though we are all seduced and distracted by the temporary pleasures of earth, "eternity is in our hearts," and nothing else will satisfy. (Ecclesiastes 3:11) Nothing outside of God's promises and desires for us will bring the satisfaction we crave.

My father had everything anyone could ask for—wealth, fame, family—yet without God what he sought after never fulfilled him. I refuse to pass on the lie. By God's grace, the curse has been broken.

Resolve to pass on the blessing of wealth that cannot be taken away—the eternal riches that cannot be seduced.

1 **What is the focus of the majority of your thoughts: self or what God is doing behind the scenes?**

How do you think these thoughts affect you?

DAY 19 The Reaction to the Action

PRINCIPLE: HOW WE RESPOND TO LIFE IS FAR MORE IMPORTANT THAN WHAT HAPPENS TO US.

How we respond to life is far more important than what happens to us.

Two people can experience identical challenges and yet respond in polar opposite ways.

Some of the most potent and memorable examples of opposite responses are found in the Bible. Elijah is known as one of the greatest prophets of all time. He prophesied that it wouldn't rain for three and a half years, and it didn't. He believed God would send ravens to feed him, and God obliged. He prophesied the miracle of God multiplying a single mother's food, and God did.

This final event is recorded in the book of 1Kings. Elijah asks a widowed mother in severe poverty to get him some water. While she is going to get it, he requests some of her bread as well.

Have you ever had a family member do that to you? As you're going to the kitchen to get something to eat, they yell, "Hey, while you're up, could you get me a glass of water… and some bread… and a napkin… and a knife… and some butter… and jelly? Hey, why don't you just stay in the kitchen until all my needs are met?"

The widow's bread just happens to be her last meal. She answers, "I do not have bread, only a handful of flour in a bin, and a little oil in a jar; and see, I am gathering a couple of sticks that I may go in and prepare it for myself and my son, that we may eat it, and die." (1Kings 17:12)

Even her hopeless response did not deter the God of Hope! (Romans 15:13) Her "Plan B" was His "Plan A." May every fatalistic perspective be removed from our hearts once and for all. "I have never seen the godly forsaken…" (Psalm 37:25) Never!

"Rest in the LORD, and wait patiently for Him." (Psalm 37:7)

He will not fail you! (1Corinthians 13:8)

1 Do you tend to be a "glass-half-full" or a "glass-half-empty" kind of person? How does this mindset affect your life?

DAY

20 When God Sunbathes

PRINCIPLE: THE SOONER YOU GIVE UP YOUR ADDICTION TO UNDERSTANDING WHAT YOU THINK IS GOING ON, THE SOONER YOU CAN REST AND TRUST GOD IN THE BLEAKEST OF SITUATIONS.

Are you a glass-is-completely-empty person?

I had a bleak roommate in college during my hippie phase. He was a completely depressed soul. He never talked and pasted dark charcoal pictures that looked like moon craters all over his closet door.

I once asked him if he was enjoying reading a certain book, just to break the two feet of solid ice in our communication. He slammed the book shut and snapped back "I wouldn't be on page 158 if I wasn't." The ice remained unbroken. I'd say he was a glass-is-completely-empty person.

When Elijah requests to eat the last meal a widow has, he then tells her, "Do not fear; go and do as you have said, but make me a small cake from it first, and bring it to me; and afterward make some for yourself and your son." (1Kings 17:13) Elijah is effectively saying, "I hear you—you're going to eat your last meal and die. That's great! While you're at it, I'll take two eggs over easy, hash browns, an English muffin and some waffles. Do you have any real butter?"

Elijah seems to be oblivious.

Do you ever feel that way about God? You are freaking out and you think all He's doing is sunbathing! Nothing could be further from the truth. Whether or not we understand it or see it, God has ordered our steps in the most marvelous way possible. The test is: will we trust what we cannot see? Frankly, will we trust God?

The Bible addresses this most clearly when it says, "Trust in the Lord with all your heart, and lean not on your own understanding; in all your ways acknowledge Him, and He shall direct your paths." (Proverbs 3:5)

The sooner we give up our addiction to understanding what we think is going on in our lives, the sooner we can rest in acknowledging and trusting God in the bleakest of situations. Only then can we experience "the peace of God, which surpasses all understanding." (Philippians 4:7)

Learning to trust God accesses the peace of mind you are looking for. It's always within reach—with arms of faith. Experience the excitement today of believing the God of the impossible. Not with presumption, based upon the desires of your heart, but upon real faith, grounded on the supreme and sublime plan of a God who loves you infinitely.

1. **Is there a situation in your life right now that you're not trusting God with?**

2. **What do you think is hindering you from trusting God in this situation?**

DAY 21

The Acceptable Year of the Lord

PRINCIPLE: MORE THAN ANYONE WHO HAS EVER KNOWN ME, GOD IS FASCINATED WITH MY LIFE.

How I perceive God's thoughts about me will affect every aspect of my life: my past, present and future. If I am so utterly unacceptable to Him, what could I possibly do to win the favor of an all-powerful God? If the One who controls my destiny is disgusted with me, then hoping for a marvelous life is wishful thinking. But, that is not the case.

One of the most refreshing revelations drawn from knowing God is realizing there is nothing I have to do to make my life special. I cannot add to my uniqueness, nor can I diminish God's one-of-a-kind plan for my life. All of His intentions toward me far exceed my expectations and, contrary to conventional wisdom, I have never disillusioned God. Why? Because He never had any illusions about me to begin with, He is fully aware of my assets and liabilities, my strengths and weaknesses.

More than anyone who has ever known me, God is fascinated with my life. This fact, when fully received, provides perhaps the greatest sigh of relief for those of us who have at one time thought we have disappointed God, believing the lie that we had to earn His approval. The truth is this: God's seal of approval is on our lives from conception to the grave. As Romans 8:35 clearly states, "nothing can separate us from the love of Christ."

Will you, today, bask in the truth that the God who is love (1John 4:8) cannot but love you? It's His very nature.

1. **What do you truly believe about God's thoughts toward you?**
2. **If these thoughts don't line up with the truth of God's Word, what is causing you to continue to believe them?**

DAY 22 The Root Issue In Life

PRINCIPLE: IF YOU WILL OBEDIENTLY DO WHAT GOD ASKS YOU TO DO, HE WILL GRACIOUSLY DO WHAT ONLY HE CAN DO.

What is the root issue in every struggle in life? Just one thing: trust.

After the impoverished single mom told Elijah she had no more food, he encouraged her with the Word of the Lord, "For thus says the Lord God of Israel: 'The bin of flour shall not be used up, nor shall the jar of oil run dry, until the day the Lord sends rain on the earth.'" (1Kings 17:14)

It takes faith, both to say this and to hear it! "So she went away and did according to the word of Elijah; and she and he and her household ate for many days." (1Kings 17:15) The widow had faith to obey the Word of the Lord, and God miraculously provided flour and oil for her.

The root issue in her life, as in ours, was trust. Was she willing to trust God to provide for her every need? If she obediently did what He asked her to do, He would graciously do what only He could.

At one point Jesus, obeying the Father, stuck his fingers in a deaf man's ears. That was big, but what followed was bigger. Jesus then took spittle and, placing it on His own fingers, put it on the man's tongue because he could not speak, either. Now, putting fingers in deaf ears and spittle on mute tongues may be just another day at the office for some people, but for most of us that level of obedience would set a world record.

Trusting God will take miraculous faith. But that, thank God, is available to all of us, if we will but ask for it.

1. **Has God ever asked something of you that seemed a bit much?**
2. **Did you obey Him? What was the outcome?**

DAY 23 Preparing for Bigger Problems Ahead

PRINCIPLE: THE CHALLENGING CIRCUMSTANCES IN YOUR LIFE ARE THE CATALYST TO GET TO YOUR ROOT PROBLEM.

Was the single mom's life in 1Kings 17 without incident from then on? Hardly! "Some time later, the son of the woman who owned the house became ill. He grew worse and worse, and finally stopped breathing." (1Kings 17:17, NIV) Now comes the bigger test!

She says to Elijah, "What do you have against me, man of God? Did you come to remind me of my sin and kill my son?" (1Kings 17:18, NIV) What is the root of this comment? Something in her past is obviously unresolved. She is still feeling guilty over a past sin. This reveals a priceless truth: when things seem to go wrong, your reaction will bring to the surface what God is really trying to get at in your life.

Whatever your challenging circumstance is, it is only the catalyst to get to the root problem. When the exasperated widow again questions Elijah, he obediently stretches out across the dead son and the boy is miraculously revived. God was not trying to torment her over past sins; He never does. He had chosen her desperate circumstances to reveal His loving heart toward her in an unforgettable way.

It is the same in our lives. God's motive is always pure. His actions are designed for our greater good; His goal is always intended to bring healing and purpose to our lives.

Your circumstances are not designed to rout your fragile life, but rather to reveal God's faithful heart. Every victory over fear, doubt, and unbelief today provides a mighty preparation for the fierce battles ahead.

1

What challenging circumstances are tempting you with thoughts of doubt and despair?

As you look through Romans 5:3–5, ask the Lord what positives have come from suffering in your life.

DAY

24 Emotional Time Bombs

PRINCIPLE: ONLY GOD CAN DEFUSE THAT WHICH CAN DESTROY ME.

The Queen Mary was the largest ship to cross the ocean in her day. When she was retired, the regal vessel was anchored as a floating hotel and museum in Long Beach, California. During the conversion process, her three massive smokestacks were taken off to be scraped down and repainted. On the dock, they each crumbled. Nothing was left of the three-quarter-inch steel plating from which the stacks had been formed. All that remained was more than 30 coats of paint, applied over many years. The steel had rusted away.

It is the same in life. Fixing surface problems will only work for so long; you have to get to the source of the problem.

Years ago in Germany, three construction workers were killed when they accidentally detonated a World War II bomb that had been lying dormant for over 50 years. We all have emotional time bombs that can sabotage us. Guilt, shame, and bitterness are lethal time bombs that, though they might seem dormant over time, eventually can (and will) explode.

The One who loves you the most desires to reveal the hidden parts of your heart that, unless healed, will explode, leaving a wake of destruction and pain. He longs to not just identify the problem, but to come with healing hands to touch your pain. Only God can defuse that which can destroy. That's why Jesus went to the Cross—to destroy the works of the enemy. (1John 3:8)

Today, would you allow the Holy Spirit to disarm and heal the explosive dimensions of your life? He will do it, if you ask, without any loss of your precious life.

1 **Ask God to show you any hidden parts of your heart (guilt, shame, bitterness, etc.) that are emotional time bombs.**

How have these hidden parts of your heart sabotaged you?

DAY 25

Humiliating Hesitations

PRINCIPLE: NO ONE ELSE COULD HAVE SAVED ME BUT THE GOD WHO CREATED ME.

Why do we hesitate to do the right thing?

I once had a soul-searching experience in a life-and-death situation. A friend's daughter had been blown out across a frigid lake in a tiny raft. Within seconds the mother selflessly dove in, risking her life to rescue her helpless child. Commitment had eclipsed contemplation. She was, as they say in poker, "All in!"

As I stood there and watched, my mind raced. Was this situation really as serious as it appeared? Was there some other willing soul who could join the desperate mother? But with seconds having passed and only a handful of people even aware a crisis was occurring, that option did not seem likely. Moments after the mother made her decision, I made mine. I dove in as well.

Yet, the mother's commitment to save her child, far more than my own commitment, resembles the sacrifice Jesus made for each of us. I would have been elated if someone—anyone—had run past me and dove into the water. But though I would have been ecstatic at the time, had the incident ended in tragedy I would have realized I had forsaken those I loved.

"Then Elijah stood in front of them [the children of Israel] and said, 'How long are you going to waver between two opinions? If the Lord is God, follow him! But if Baal is God, then follow him!' But the people were completely silent." (1Kings 18:21, NLT)

Since receiving God's love for my life, I have committed my heart fully to Him. No one else could have saved me but the God who created me, for only He was willing to pay the price of rescuing my tortured soul.

1. **What causes you to sometimes hesitate to do the right thing?**

2. **Do you hesitate to share about what the Lord has done in your life because of fear or possible embarrassment?**

DAY 26

Apologizing For My Life

PRINCIPLE: KNOWING GOD TRULY LIKES YOU WILL AFFECT EVERY ASPECT OF YOUR LIFE.

When you're alone with God, what does He think of you?

As a lover of Jesus for more than three decades, I have had many tranquil moments watching ocean waves at sunset, reflecting on the wonders of God. Many times, these moments have been the perfect therapy for my battle-weary soul. However, on occasion, I have ended up more apologetic than refreshed. My time of prayer would invariably conclude with, "God, I love you, and I thank you for loving me. You have blessed my life in so many ways. I am eternally grateful. But, God, as I look at my many shortcomings, I just want to say, I'm sorry. I know I haven't been all that You intended me to be. I know my character has at times failed and I just want to again say, I'm so very sorry."

At that emotional crescendo I would often begin to sob, devastated to think my life had not measured up to the way God wanted it to turn out. I found myself always falling short of my perception of God's expectation for my life, regardless of whether I was in a season of spiritual victory or setbacks. This prayer of apology always left me feeling inadequate and empty.

Years later, after a momentous breakthrough in my understanding, I have at last embraced the truth of God's heart toward me. One moment before I received Jesus, He was madly in love with me. A few moments later, I had been transformed, but He had not changed at all. He was still completely and totally in love with me. This truth has set me free, and now stands as an immoveable pillar in my relationship with God.

If you do not know that God is head-over-heals in love with you, ask Him to reveal this transforming reality. Once you know He truly likes you, your perspective concerning every aspect of your life will never be the same.

1. Have you had moments in which you apologized to God for your inadequacies?

2. How would your perspective of life change if you embraced the fact that God's love for you is unwavering?

   Look through the lens of John 3:16, and ask God to show you how much He loves you.

DAY

27 Why So Critical?

PRINCIPLE: THE GREATEST JOY IN GOD THE FATHER'S HEART IS KNOWING THAT WE, HIS SONS AND DAUGHTERS, ARE ABSOLUTELY CONVINCED HE IS NOT DISAPPOINTED IN WHO WE ARE.

Though a faultfinding view of ourselves may in some neurotic way fulfill the letter of the law, it is by no means the truth. Healthy parents do not relish in their child's incessant apologies for not being the son or daughter they had hoped for. In the same way, God does not get joy out of my apologizing for my life. If after a child's failing to live up to expectations, the default emotion to surface in the parents' and child's communication is disappointment, something is seriously wrong.

Throughout most of my life, because I never fulfilled my natural father's massive expectations for me, I assumed that God the Father must have felt the same way. Now I know that, though I am a sinner and my sins have hurt God, my failures alone do not sum up my relationship with Him—far from it.

His Word promises that when we truly receive what Christ's death and resurrection have accomplished, we are forever separated from the consequences of our sins, including guilt, shame and condemnation. "As far as the east is from the west, so far has He removed our transgressions from us." (Psalm 103:12)

Since we will spend eternity focusing on what God did right on our behalf, not what we did wrong, we should embrace this eternal perspective today. The greatest joy of our heavenly Father's heart is knowing that we, His sons and daughters, are absolutely convinced He is not disappointed in who we are, but, like any doting father, He is proud to call us His own.

1. **Do you feel like a disappointment to God? If so, how does this affect your relationship with Him?**
2. **Look through the lens of Psalm 103:12, and embrace what God has done on your behalf.**

DAY 28

Compensating For Our Past

PRINCIPLE: ONLY BY CONNECTING WITH GOD'S DEPTHLESS, UNCONDITIONAL LOVE CAN YOU PROCESS LIFE AS GOD INTENDED.

None of us are capable of compensating for our past. Therefore, God in His mercy promises us, "I, even I, am He who blots out your transgressions for My own sake; and I will not remember your sins." (Isaiah 43:25) Unlike us, God can make this claim and actually fulfill His promise every time.

1John 1:9 asserts, "If we confess our sins, He is faithful and just to forgive us our sins and to cleanse us from all unrighteousness." Understanding the meaning of life has little to do with how much we love God, but it has everything to do with how much He loves us. My love fluctuates; His love is unwavering.

Jesus affirmed this truth when He openly confessed, "As the Father loved Me, I also have loved you; abide in My love." (John 15:9) We are as loved by the Father as Jesus was. And He longs for us to remain in a constant connection with this depthless, unconditional love. Only then can we process life as God intended. There is nothing more tragic than being unwilling or unable to fully receive the love God so longs to give us. He alone gave everything to demonstrate how deeply He loves and cares.

Today, if you have any un-confessed sin, confess it, and receive God's complete forgiveness. After doing so, believe that you have been fully released from not just the penalty of your sin, but also from any distance between you and God.

You are as cherished by the Father as Jesus. You are as much a delight to Him as His first-born Son.Spending your day believing this truth is infinitely more pleasing to God than believing the lie that you are in some way a disappointment to Him.

Do you feel cherished by God? How does that affect you?

1 **Look through the lens of 1John 1:8–9, confess any un-confessed sin and receive God's complete forgiveness.**

DAY

29 God Likes You

PRINCIPLE: GOD ALWAYS LOOKS FORWARD TO BEING WITH YOU, AND IS NEVER DISAPPOINTED IN WHO YOU ARE.

Do you know that God likes you, not just loves you?

Realizing this truth will open up a whole new relationship with Him.

Since the International House of Prayer (IHOP) in Kansas City inaugurated non-stop prayer and worship in September 1999, thousands have been drawn there, spending hour after hour soaking in the presence of God. During my week long visits in early 2003, as I spent many hours saturated in God's Spirit at IHOP, God did a revolutionary work in my heart. I experienced a closeness to Jesus I had not felt since I was a brand new Christian, some 30 years earlier.

I spent countless hours basking in the wonderful presence of God. There were powerful teachings about God's fascination for us: how He longs for His sons and daughters, and how we, the Bride of Christ, captivate His heart. Over time, these teachings opened my eyes to see that God doesn't just love us; He genuinely likes and enjoys us immensely.

In the deepest part of my being I sensed God's heart was completely accepting, with no disappointment or sense of failure—only the joy of a lost son being fully restored to his Father. All I could do was receive God's loving embrace, and as I did, something extraordinary took place.

For years, even decades, I had developed a pattern of expressing my love to God. Many times throughout the day I would say, "God, I love you," or "Thank you, Jesus, for loving and caring for my life." I had considered this my First Love relationship with Jesus. In reality, it was Second Love. His love for me came first.

The Bible says, "We love Him because He first loved us." (1John 4:19) I had become so preoccupied trying to attain God's approval; I had lost sight of His unwavering acceptance. Actually, I had never fully realized the extent of His feelings toward me.

It is not just a joy to be in God's presence, but He finds it a joy to be in our presence.

Today, ask God to reveal this magnificent truth to you. Then, whenever you come into His presence, you will rejoice to know He always looks forward to being with you and is never disappointed in who you are.

Do you believe that you make God smile?
If so, bask in this truth. If not, then why not?

1 **Look through the lens of 1John 4:19, and ask God you to show you His steadfast love and acceptance of you.**

DAY 30 You Make God Smile

PRINCIPLE: GOD TAKES PLEASURE IN THE VERY THOUGHT OF YOU.

How can you fully love God if you don't know He fully likes you?

Over time I have learned to lean less on the commitment I have made to Jesus, and to bask more in the eternal covenant He has made with me. John, the beloved disciple, qualifies the essential sequence of love: "This is real love. It is not that we loved God, but that He loved us and sent His Son as a sacrifice to take away our sins." (1John 4:10, NLT)

I now discipline my spirit and soul to receive His unconditional love for me. I reject any thought that conflicts with the ultimate thought: that God is madly in love with me no matter what I have done or what sin I have committed.

There is nothing I could ever do to make God stop loving me.

My repentance and return to God does not reactivate His love for me. It was never deactivated. Even before I was born, His thoughts toward me were pure joy and gladness.

How can I fully love God if I don't know He fully loves me? As Jack Frost taught, "God loves you the way you are, and not the way you think you should be." If I sense He is actually displeased with me, then others will eventually sense I am displeased with them. I cannot give more than I have received. I cannot pass on to my children more than I have, whatever it may be: love, peace, joy, forgiveness, mercy, kindness, or acceptance. Kind will produce kind. Acceptance will produce acceptance.

King David once wrote, "How precious [valuable] are Your thoughts about me, O God! They are innumerable!" (Psalms 139:17, NLT) God sees us as precious, even priceless. Before we were born and throughout our lives, He continues to have an infinite number of positive thoughts about us. As a truly caring parent, He adores us.

The Bible teaches that God the Father loves us no less than He loves His Son Jesus. In the Gospel of John, Jesus said, "As the Father loved Me, I also have loved you; abide in My love." (John 15:9) Likewise in the words of Jesus, "You have sent Me, and have loved them as You have loved Me." (John 17:23b) Ever see doting parents smile at their child? That's how God feels about us. God takes pleasure in the very thought of us. We make God smile!

Believe it. Speak it. Cherish it. It is a truth that will set you free.

1 **What thoughts tend to come into your mind about the way God thinks about you?**

2 **How do these thoughts affect you and your relationship with Him?**

Look through the lens of John 17:23b, and rewrite it with your name inserted. Believe it. Speak it. Cherish it.

DAY 31 The Greatest Revelation I Never Had

PRINCIPLE: IF YOU HAVE EVER BELIEVED GOD LOVED YOU, OR EVEN LIKED YOU, HE STILL DOES.

Do you live like God likes you?

When my heart began to soak in the life-transforming truth that God liked me, I disciplined my mind to stop chanting, "I love you, God!" This expression seemed, for some tragic reason, to beg the question, "God, do you really love me too?" As my soul focused on His unconditional love for me, I was captivated by God's heart. It sounds like a simple enough revelation, but one I frankly never fully grasped.

A few weeks after an eventful trip to IHOP (International House of Prayer), while spending time with our pastoral team overlooking the Pacific Ocean in northern California, I realized my heart had been changed. Gone was the apologetic view of my sorry little life. I no longer felt the compulsion to close my prayers saddened by what I had not become. At last, I realized there was nothing I could ever do to make God love me more. Likewise, there was nothing I could ever do to make Him love me less. His loving-kindness toward me was unshakeable.

I am now fully convinced that God likes me, even though in my immaturity I do things He doesn't like and I know are wrong. God could not love me any more than He already does. He does not love me more when I am good, nor does He love me any less when I am bad. Even in my lowest moments God still likes me and fully differentiates between who I am and what I do.

Like a good parent, His love for me is unwavering. The Bible says He is the same "yesterday, today, and forever," (Hebrews 13:8) and, "For I am the Lord, I do not change." (Malachi 3:6a) Therefore, if you have ever believed God loved you, or even liked you, He still does. He cannot change. He has not moved His affections from you. God likes you all the time just as you are, not based upon your performance, but based upon who He created you to be.

Mike Bickle sums this up so well in his book, The Pleasures of Loving God; "God doesn't see us the way many of us see ourselves. He does not define us by our struggles, but rather He defines us by His passion for us and our longing to be a lover of God."

Every gift God has for you must be received by faith—even the conviction that He is passionately in love with you. Today, fight to believe this truth and you will, once and for all, discern God's infinite love for you.

Do you think God likes you?

1 Look through the lens of Hebrews 13:8, and ask yourself what it means to you that God's affections toward you never change.

DAY 32 Whose Opinion of Me Matters Most?

PRINCIPLE: GOD'S THOUGHTS ABOUT ME ARE ALL THAT REALLY MATTER.

Before we can fully appreciate the fact that God genuinely likes us, we have to understand who He really is. If we fail to see Him as the kind of person we would want to like us, then it really doesn't make a difference what He thinks?

When I was a young Christian, there was a woman living in our community who personally knew Charles Manson, a cult leader and mass murderer during the 1970s. After some discussion and prayer, we decided to write Manson a letter in prison, trying to share the love of Jesus with him. Within days he sent back a surprisingly lengthy response, attempting to persuade us that he was the savior we were looking for, not Jesus. It would have been laughable if it weren't so sad. Was it hard for us to reject Charles Manson's invitation to follow him? Not at all! I didn't care what he thought of me, because I thought so little of his opinion.

On the other hand, our Creator is the only person truly worthy of our complete allegiance and affection. (Matthew 22:37) His thoughts about us are all that really matter. Do we know what God really thinks of us? Is He glad or sad, grateful or disappointed in whom we have become? The answer to this question will shape every dimension of our lives and could not possibly be overestimated.

We are God's sons and daughters. If we believe He is ashamed of who we are, we will walk in shame. On the other hand, if we believe God created us in His image and likeness, (Genesis 1:26) then we can walk in confidence and security, knowing we are accepted by the One who matters the most. Not only does Jesus accept us without reservation, He willingly chose to give His life so that we might have life. (John 20:31)

Do you think God is glad or sad, grateful or disappointed in whom you have become?

1

Look through the lens of John 20:31, and meditate on what type of love would motivate the Lord to willingly give His life for you?

DAY

33 God Wants to Crown You

PRINCIPLE: NO MATTER WHAT SINS OR MISTAKES YOU HAVE MADE IN LIFE, IT IS ESSENTIAL THAT YOU FULLY ACCEPT THE TRUTH THAT GOD DOES NOT WANT TO CLOBBER YOU. HE WANTS TO CROWN YOU!

"You shall also be a crown of glory in the hand of the Lord, and a royal diadem in the hand of your God. You shall no longer be termed Forsaken ['destitute, refuse'], nor shall your land any more be termed Desolate ['devastated, wasted']; but you shall be called Hephzibah ['a pleasure, desirable, a valuable thing, acceptable, delightsome'], and your land Beulah ['married, a wife']. For the Lord delights in you, and your land shall be married." (Isaiah 62:3–4)

The crowning moment of my life was the realization that I was no longer forsaken, devastated, and wasted, but that my life was actually a pleasure to God, valuable, accepted, and a delight.

I was created to be the Bride of His dreams, not the embodiment of His disappointment.

What a relief!

What a joy!

We will never know the fullness of God's love until we experience failure and then realize He is still madly in love with us.

"Thanks be to God for His indescribable gift!" (2Corinthians 9:15)

1. What would disqualify you from being crowned as God intended?

2. Can you see that Jesus died to liberate you from even that?

DAY 34

Misunderstanding The Love Of God

PRINCIPLE: MY EXPRESSING HOW MUCH I LOVE GOD COULD NOT POSSIBLY HAVE THE SAME EFFECT AS RECEIVING HIS LOVE FOR ME.

Can your love for God ever compete with His love for you?

Prior to the revelation of God liking me, I suffered from a glaring misunderstanding of scripture related to the love of God. Whenever I read about the love of God in the Bible, I would consistently think of my love for God.

When I would read Romans 5:5, which says, "Now hope does not disappoint, because the love of God has been poured out in our hearts by the Holy Spirit who was given to us," I would think, "my hope will not be disappointed if I continue to demonstrate my love for God." My thinking was totally flawed. I now believe this scripture could more accurately be interpreted as, "I can be hopeful in every situation because God's everlasting love continues to be poured out in my heart by the Holy Spirit."

With the revelation of God liking me, I came to the realization that the emphasis should never have been on my love for God, but instead, always and in every situation, on His love for me. There is an infinite difference between my capacity to hold on to God and His commitment and ability to hold on to me.

Take a look at Jude 1:21: "Keep yourselves in the love of God, looking for the mercy of our Lord Jesus Christ unto eternal life." This verse encourages me that if I continue to receive God's love for my life, I will remain face to face with the eternal mercy of God found most evidently in the life and death of the Lord Jesus Christ.

My attempts to remain focused on my love for God will lead once again to a roller coaster of disappointment in my own imperfections.

During that transitional season of my life, I continuously readjusted my thoughts to receive God's Word as He intended. I even disciplined myself to not tell God I loved Him. My chanting, "I love you, God!" had become a subconscious attempt at trying to retain His acceptance. In reality, my expressing how much I loved God could not possibly have the same effect as first receiving His love for me.

Over time, as my heart was healed, and I was able to more fully embrace God's overwhelming love for me. I began to express my love for God once again, but only after being fully saturated in His First Love for me.

Oswald Chambers sums up this principle so well when he writes, "The only relationship God wants to have with us is based on love; if we refuse these terms, there is no relationship."

1. **How would you describe the difference between God's love for you and your love for God?**

2. **How does realizing that God loved you first affect you?**

   Look through the lens of Romans 5:5.

3. **How does this affect your hopefulness in every life situation?**

DAY 35

Receiving God's Approval

PRINCIPLE: I WAS CREATED TO BE THE BRIDE OF HIS DREAMS, NOT THE EMBODIMENT OF HIS DISAPPOINTMENT.

How many young women have given away their emotions, their trust, their intimacy, and even their moral purity, desperately wanting someone to love and completely approve of them?

How many men, likewise, have done things they knew were wrong just to impress someone?

Today's cultural seal of approval is centered on the applause of men, having a shelf life measured in nanoseconds compared to eternity. We can spend our lives endlessly attempting to derive our value from a fallen planet hurdling toward judgment for its self-obsession, or we can choose to build on what is consistent with God's Word and is guaranteed to last forever.

We see our immense value to God most clearly in the life of Jesus. Jesus began His earthly ministry at age 30. When John the Baptist baptized Him in the Jordan River, a supernatural event took place that reveals the Father's heart for each of us. "Jesus came up immediately from the water; and behold, the heavens were opened to Him, and He saw the Spirit of God descending like a dove and alighting upon Him. And suddenly a voice came from Heaven, saying, 'This is My beloved Son, in whom I am well pleased.' " (Matthew 3:16b–17)

There is no evidence in Scripture prior to this event that the Father had spoken audibly to Jesus during His first 30 years on this Earth. For His coming out party, God the Father had a special treat. He wanted everyone to know how proud He was of His Son, so He shouted from Heaven, "Hey everybody, listen up, this is My Son; and, 'You know what, Son? I really love You and am so very proud of you!'" The Father broke His three decades of silence to share two life-changing principles: "I love You, and I am so very proud of You."

Most of us have never been overly concerned about whether the Father loved or was proud of Jesus. We all pretty much assume, "What's not to like?" But the love and approval the Father bestowed on Jesus was not reserved for Him alone. In Ephesians 1:6, the Word of God promises us as well, "…He [God] made us accepted in the Beloved." Here "Beloved" is derived from the same Greek word used when referring to Jesus as Beloved in Matthew 3:17. Thus, we are accepted into the same Beloved family as Jesus.

In a very real sense, when our lives are surrendered to Jesus, the Father likewise speaks from Heaven to each of us, "Hey, listen up, this is My child. And you know what? I really love you and am so very proud of you!" What a comfort to know we are as much loved and approved of by God as Jesus.

1. **How have you been affected when you have failed and then been rejected?**

2. **What impact does it have on you to realize that God's love and approval for you is constant, and you are valuable, accepted and a delight?**

   Look through the lens of Ephesians 1:5–6, and be encouraged because you are as much loved and approved of by God as Jesus.

DAY 36

Smiling With His Spirit

PRINCIPLE: NO MATTER WHO I AM OR WHAT I HAVE DONE, I NEED TO KNOW THAT THERE'S A GOD WHO NOT ONLY LOVES ME UNCONDITIONALLY, BUT LIKES ME COMPLETELY.

During the mid-19th century, a boy named Joseph seemed completely normal until age two when abrasions began to appear on his skin. They were the first swells of a violent storm that would envelope his fragile life.

Joseph had a wonderful, Godly mother, but she died when he was ten years old. He was left with a cruel father and a bitter stepmother who hated him. Joseph's deformities worsened. He had massive feet, was unable to use one of his hands, and became deaf in one ear and blind in one eye. The malformation of his mouth made it almost impossible to understand him when he talked.

At one point, his head measured three feet in circumference, his right wrist twelve inches, and his right thumb five inches. Fungus grew all over his body, giving him a hideous odor. As a teenager, Joseph was so deformed that while he tried to sell products door to door, women would scream and even faint.

When Joseph was 15, his alcoholic father beat him so badly he was left unconscious and bleeding underneath the kitchen table. Sometime during the night, Joseph regained consciousness, crawled out from beneath the table, and quietly gathered a few belongings, leaving home for good. Unable to support himself, the dejected youth eventually found work in a freak show—billed as "Joseph Merrick—The Elephant Man." Because his skin looked like elephant skin, his handlers made up a story that while his mother was pregnant with him, an elephant had attacked her.

One day, a doctor visited him and, overcome with compassion, placed Joseph in a hospital. The doctor later described Joseph as "the most disgusting specimen of humanity I have ever seen." During this period of his life, when one of the hospital attendants smiled at Joseph, he was so overcome by the kindness of this simple act that he broke down in tears saying, "You are the first woman I can ever remember who smiled at me."

During his long hospital stay, to the amazement of everyone around him, Joseph built incredibly elaborate cathedral-like structures using only one hand. He would sit and read the Bible, especially the Psalms, for hours. It was said of Joseph, “He could not smile with his face, but he learned to smile with his spirit.”

At just 28 years of age, Joseph passed away, having lived a truly extraordinary life. In spite of overwhelmingly tragic circumstances, Joseph learned something that many people with far easier lives never do. He learned that God really liked him, and he was able to live in the joy and peace that comes from this life-altering revelation. As I reflect on his broken life, I like to imagine he once read and believed the comforting words of King David, “this I know…God is for me.” (Psalms 56:9b)

No matter who we are or what we have done, whether beautiful or ugly, rich or poor, good or bad, loved or unloved, approved or rejected, we each must know in the deepest part of our being that there is a God who made us in His own image and likeness. A God who not only loves us unconditionally, but likes us so completely His heart smiles every time He thinks of us—and He thinks of us constantly.

1

In what ways does it affect you to realize that God's heart is smiling every time He thinks of you?

Look through the lens of Psalm 56:9b, and meditate on what this promise means to you?

DAY

37 Misplaced Blame

PRINCIPLE: ONE OF THE GREATEST REVELATIONS YOU WILL EVER HAVE IS REALIZING YOU ALONE ARE RESPONSIBLE FOR HOW YOU CHOOSE TO RESPOND TO LIFE.

Much of my childhood was something I would rather forget. Once, when I was 15, the oppressive religious school I attended had a one-day retreat for my entire class. While there, each student was asked to spend time alone in a rose garden talking with God about His plans for our lives. It was the last thing I wanted to do! As far as I was concerned, God had ceased to exist. I figured if He wasn't the perpetrator of my miserable life, He certainly drove the getaway car.

Nothing could calm the fury of my hurt and hostility toward an absentee God. My reluctant stroll around the garden was short and bitter. At one point I told God, "If You are responsible for what's happening in my life, then we have nothing in common. This is my final conversation with You!" And for seven years, it was.

How much mileage can you get out of blaming others for your life, whether it's people or God? Not much! At some point you will run out of gas and realize you alone are responsible for how you choose to respond to life. Ultimately, the condition of my heart and mind is my own choice. I let my indignation over the massive amount of hurts blind my ability to see what God was actually doing in my life. One day, I would learn to lay aside my selfish desires for a God who longed to give me greater understanding of His perfect plan and heal my broken heart.

Years later, God dropped this verse into my broken heart, "Even if my father and mother abandon me, the LORD will hold me close." (Psalm 27:10, NLT) He has been faithful to keep this promise.

1. **Do you blame God, or others, for any discouraging times in your past?**

2. **Are you now ready to stop blaming and take responsibility for the condition of your heart and mind?**

DAY 38

Always Going Through It... Never Going Under

PRINCIPLE: REFUSE TO BLAME GOD FOR YOUR DIFFICULTIES.

What would it take for you to never be discouraged again?

It's more than possible; it's God's will. If you can believe it.

In the New Testament, the Apostle Paul was a revolutionary preacher who lived an extremely challenging life. He gave up much to follow Jesus, and though he continually met with seemingly insurmountable challenges, he refused to blame God for his difficulties. Unlike most of us, he did not allow himself to become angry or bitter with God because the conditions of his life were often miserable.

In the beginning of 2Corinthians 12, Paul is taken to Heaven and receives such mind-expanding revelations that he is never permitted to speak of them again. The apostle sees and hears so many lofty things, he is concerned he will be overcome with pride.

Paul plainly states, "And lest I should be exalted above measure by the abundance of the revelations, a thorn in the flesh was given to me, a messenger of Satan to [torment] me..." (2Corinthians 12:7) Paul has gone from being elated about spiritual revelations to begging God for help, "Concerning this thing I pleaded with the Lord three times that it might depart from me." (2Corinthians 12:8)

Was Paul just a coward unwilling to fight his own battles? Not at all! He could take a hit as well as anyone who ever lived. In fact, in the previous chapter he lists just some of the greatest tests of his life, "From the Jews five times I received forty stripes minus one. Three times I was beaten with rods; once I was stoned [being hit with rocks thrown by an angry mob and left for dead], three times I was shipwrecked; a night and a day I have been in the deep; in journeys often, in perils of waters, in perils of robbers, in perils of my own countrymen, in perils of the Gentiles, in perils in the city, in perils in the wilderness, in perils in the sea, in perils among false brethren; in weariness and toil, in sleeplessness often, in hunger and thirst, in fastings often, in cold and nakedness..." (2Corinthians 11:24–27)

Paul wasn't some lightweight, unwilling to deal with hard situations. He was a gnarly street fighter who followed Jesus regardless of the cost, yet he begged God to remove the thorn from his side. What was God's response to Paul's desperate pleadings? Did He issue an edict to stop the satanic tormenting? Hardly. God's response seemed to bring NO immediate relief whatsoever.

Paul wrote, "And [God] said to me, 'My grace is sufficient for you, for My strength is made perfect in weakness.' Therefore most gladly I will rather boast in my infirmities, that the power of Christ may rest upon me." (2Corinthians 12:9) In this case, the original Greek word for infirmities means feebleness (of mind or body), a malady, a physical or psychological disorder, disease, frailty, sickness, or weakness.

Paul understood that God's all-sufficient grace was being poured out.

It was all he needed to fight discouragement.

Frankly, it's all we need today as well.

1. **Have you ever felt like the Lord wasn't listening to your cries for help?**

   How did that affect you?

2. **What do you think your life would look like if you chose never to be discouraged again?**

   As you look through the lens of 2Corinthians 12:9–10, reflect upon what the Lord is promising you within every discouraging situation.

DAY

39 The Key to Contentment

PRINCIPLE: CONTENTMENT IS THE RESULT OF TRUSTING GOD NO MATTER WHAT IS HAPPENING AROUND YOU.

What would you give to have perfect contentment, every moment, in every situation, for the rest of your life?

Paul the Apostle once placed a new understanding as a permanent filter guiding every dimension of his life. He wrote, "...I take pleasure in [Greek—'think well of, approve, am pleased with'] infirmities, in reproaches ['insults, hurts'] in needs, in persecutions, in distresses ['calamities, anguish'] for Christ's sake. For when I am weak, then I am strong." (2Corinthians 12:10)

Here's Paul's radical, groundbreaking perspective: "I'm going to see God working in every situation of my life. I'm going to think well of every circumstance. I may be sick, hurt or insulted; I may have massive needs, persecutions, distresses, calamities and anguish. But, no matter what happens, I'm not going to forget this one thing: as weak as I feel, I will learn to rely on God for strength. He will see me through."

Because of this astounding, life-changing epiphany, after being beaten and thrown into jail, in the book of Philippians Paul was able to affirm, "I have learned in whatever state I am, there I will be content." (Philippians 4:11) What a discovery! He is declaring, "My contentment has nothing to do with what is happening around me, and everything to do with what is happening inside me."

Contentment is the result of our trusting God no matter what is happening around us. It is more of a decision than a consequence. It is the antithesis of the victim mindset, and it is the dawn of a new era of personal responsibility. Paul had the breakthrough of a lifetime because he was willing to continually die to his own misconceptions of God.

1 **What could you begin to do to deepen your trust in God in every situation?**

DAY 40

Challenging the Greatest

PRINCIPLE: GOD DOESN'T DISQUALIFY YOU. BELIEVING THIS IS A NECESSARY PART OF ESTABLISHING A RELATIONSHIP BASED UPON TRUST.

Have you ever said, "God, why are you doing this to me?"

In the New Testament, John the Baptist, like each of us, struggled at times with seeing God at work in his life.

From his mother's womb, John knew who Jesus was. When John was baptizing in the Jordan River and saw Jesus coming, he said, "Behold! The Lamb of God who takes away the sins of the world!" (John 1:29) John recognized Jesus as the Son of God, both in the womb and as an adult.

Some time later, when John was in prison and about to be beheaded, he sent a few of his disciples to ask Jesus, "Are You the Coming One, or do we look for another?" (Luke 7:20) Was John suffering from amnesia, or frightened by the eminency of his death? Or, perhaps like us at times, was he merely questioning, "God, where are You?"

Who was John the Baptist anyway? Was he some unstable, erratic eccentric, or one of the most solid and focused prophetic voices in all of human history? Jesus once said of his cousin John, "among those born of women there is not a greater prophet than John the Baptist…" (Luke 7:28) John was one of the premiere prophets of all time. And yet, in the hour of his greatest temptation, John may have questioned if Jesus really was the Messiah.

Questioning God doesn't disqualify us. It's a necessary part of developing a relationship based upon trust—proving God is Who He says He is.

1 Have you ever wondered where God was during a challenging situation?

____

____

____

DAY 41 Questioning God

PRINCIPLE: ONE OF THE GREATEST CHALLENGES IN LIFE IS NOT BEING OFFENDED WITH GOD.

With perhaps the exception of the Josephs and Daniels, it is hard to find a prophet, judge, king, or apostle who was not at times bewildered as to God's intention. Since most of us have cried out, "God where are you? What's going on in my life?" we should never look down upon others when they are in this valley of despair.

Even the great prophet Elijah had his moments of vacillation. Having just miraculously called down fire from Heaven and killed 450 prophets of Baal, he was overcome with fear, hid in a cave, and wanted to die because King Ahab's wife Jezebel had vowed to kill him. (1Kings 18–19)

In the New Testament, it was no less than Jesus Himself who compared John the Baptist to Elijah, "And if you are willing to receive and accept it, John himself is Elijah who was to come [before the kingdom]." (Matthew 11:14, Amplified) Perhaps these two of history's greatest men had more similarities than some of us would like to acknowledge? They both questioned God at a low-point in their lives.

After establishing for John's disciples His credentials as a healer and deliverer in Luke 7, Jesus follows up with an extraordinarily revealing statement. He challenges John with, "And blessed is he who is not offended because of Me…." (Luke 7:23) Jesus is in essence saying, "Blessed is he who is not offended in the things I put him through." Another translation would be, "Happy and to be envied are those who refuse to question God in the hour of their greatest personal pain." Quite a statement! Certainly rich with implications when spoken to a man who would soon have his head chopped off.

If you are questioning God, wait patiently upon Him. Just up ahead a new understanding will bring the clarity you've been waiting for.

1 Do you think God's dealt you a rotten hand?

DAY

42 Whine Flu

PRINCIPLE: WILL I LIVE A LIFE WHINING ABOUT WHAT DIDN'T HAPPEN, OR REJOICING IN WHAT DID?

At the end of my life, will I have seen all that took place from God's eternal viewpoint, or merely the myopic shallowness of Earth? Will I whine about what didn't happen or rejoice in what did? I can begin to choose which understanding I want to have today. Tomorrow will be here before I know it.

When King David was facing death due to old age, his parting words give us a glimpse into his view of God's faithfulness during his remarkable life, "As the Lord lives, who has redeemed my life from every distress..." (1Kings 1:29) Did God actually rescue David every time? David had conquered both the wrath of the Philistine giant Goliath and the treachery of the psychotic King Saul. Like Jesus, when betrayed by those closest to Him, David was given wisdom to overcome the bitterness of his wife Michal and the deception of his son Absalom. Though David failed miserably at times as a husband and father, and was even guilty of the heinous crimes of murder and adultery, God redeemed every ugly situation in David's life for His glory, saying, "I have found David, the son of Jesse, a man after My own heart, who will do all My will." (Acts 13:22b)

I want to be someone after God's heart, who will do all of His will. May God cover my failings with His blood, and remove the whining from my heart, replacing it with rejoicing. For God have been good to me—infinitely better than I deserve. "May the words of my mouth and the thoughts of my heart be pleasing to You, O LORD, my rock and my redeemer." (Psalm 19:14, NLT)

Do you tend to whine about what didn't happen, or rejoice about what did?

1

Look through the lens of Psalm 19:14, and ask the Lord to remove the whining from your heart and replace it with rejoicing.

DAY

43 Dead Man Walking

PRINCIPLE: THE ONLY PEOPLE WHO DON'T GET OVERWHELMED BY LIFE ARE DEAD.

How should you respond to the greatest difficulties in life?

David wrote part of his secret in the Psalms, "The Lord says, 'Be still and know that I am God.' " (Psalms 46:10) When are we most still? When we are sleeping? No. Replays reveal most people toss and turn.

All of us are most still when we are dead. Try to irritate a dead person and he won't even look at you; jump on his head—again, complete indifference. Temptations mean nothing to him, nor does any amount of peer pressure. Why? Because he's dead—dead to fear, dead to worry, dead to anger, and dead to lust. He's beyond the seductions of this earth. You could paraphrase Psalm 46:10, "Drop dead and know that I am God."

All of us want resurrection life, but we will never have it until we are dead to ourselves. Paul never said, "I die monthly when the bills come in" or "I die yearly during tax season." No, he proclaimed, "I die daily." (1Corinthians 15:31) He essentially said, "I'm a dead man, walking!"

How often should we die to our ambitions, our self-will, and even ourselves? Resurrection life is only available to dead people. If Jesus had to die to get it, so do we. But His promise to us is sure, "if the Spirit of Him who raised Jesus from the dead dwells in you, He who raised Christ from the dead will also give life to your mortal bodies through His Spirit who dwells in you." (Romans 8:11)

How can you tell if you are dead to yourself? When you are asleep in a boat in the middle of a storm. When someone slaps you on one cheek, and you turn the other one. When all Hell is breaking loose outside of you, and Heaven keeps rising in you.

1. **In what ways do you die to self, daily?**

DAY

44 Loving Strangers

PRINCIPLE: THE ONE WE EACH REJECTED BY COUNTLESS SELFISH ACTS WILLINGLY SACRIFICED HIMSELF FOR US.

Does your love have limits?

I once read a short newspaper article about a couple in North Carolina. Jerry and Dolores Burdette were newly married and had everything to live for. One day, as they walked along a beach, they heard cries for help coming from the churning surf. Four people were drowning. The first had been helplessly captured by the undertow; one by one each of the others had entered the water to help, only to be sucked into the undertow as well. All four were fighting for their lives.

As soon as Jerry saw their predicament, he dove in as well. An excellent swimmer, Jerry reached the closest person and brought him safely to shore. He then dove back in and rescued the second and then the third. Completely exhausted, but seeing the plight of the fourth drowning soul, Jerry, without regard for his own safety, swam back outland grabbed hold of the last person. Though Jerry was able to get the final victim close enough to shore to make it back on his own, he himself was so depleted of strength he was unable to continue. Jerry sank out of sight as his precious bride watched, having given his life for four complete strangers.

I have often thought of that brave, faceless man and wondered what happened to his wife Dolores and those four people Jerry died for. What responsibility had any of the four taken for Dolores' life? They were drowning in a violent ocean and a passerby gave his life to rescue them. As each one crawled onto the shore and greeted his wife, I can't imagine they would walk away having only thanked her half-heartedly. Her husband had died to save each of them and in doing so her life was forever changed. Her wellbeing should, in some way, be their responsibility because the one she lived for had given his life for them. I have prayed for Dolores on a number of occasions that her life would be doubly blessed. She had married a noble man, who selflessly gave his life for others.

We see this same principle in the life of Jesus. All of us were drowning in an ocean of sin, incapable of saving ourselves, when the God of the Universe—the One we had each rejected by countless selfish acts—willingly sacrificed Himself for us. He died on a cross in the most brutal way imaginable just so we might live with Him forever. How grateful should we be to a God for such a selfless action? Spending eternity thanking and praising Him would still pale in comparison to what He gave for each of us. Jesus underscored the cost of love when he said, "Greater love has no one than this, than to lay down one's life for his friends." (John 15:13) Jesus, thank You for laying Your life down for us.

1. **Would you lay down your life for a stranger?**
2. **How can you lay down your life for a stranger today?**

DAY

45 Forgiven Much?

PRINCIPLE: IF WE ARE TRULY FORGIVEN, WE SHOULD BE AS GRATEFUL AS A PERSON WHO HAS JUST BEEN RESCUED FROM A HORRIBLE DEATH.

If you were short one penny and the sales person said, "Go ahead, take a penny," would your eyes well up with tears for his generosity? Would you then say," I will never forget you for as long as I live!" No, it was just a penny. The extent to which we have been rescued is the extent to which we should be grateful.

In the Gospel of Luke, an immoral woman came to a house where Jesus was staying. Weeping and kneeling beside Jesus, she washed His dirty feet with her tears. As those around her looked on in astonishment, she wiped His feet with her hair, continually kissing and anointing them with expensive perfume. Seeing this shocking display of affection, one hypocritical Pharisee spoke to himself saying, "This Man, if He were a prophet, would know who and what manner of woman this is who is touching Him, for she is a sinner.'" (Luke 7:39) Jesus, however, knew his thoughts and replied, "...her sins, which are many, are forgiven, for she loved much. But to whom little is forgiven, the same loves little." (Luke 7:47)

Being a little sinner is like being a little pregnant—you either are or you're not. If you are forgiven, then you're completely forgiven. If we are truly forgiven, we should be as grateful as a person who has just been rescued from a horrible death. Paul wrote, "For to me, to lives Christ, and to die is gain." (Philippians 1:21) He was, in essence, saying that there are two marvelous options for each of us: life or death. Make today a win win day. Die to self, and be alive to Jesus.

1 Is your life transparent for others to see? Why?

DAY 46

Realizing Your Destiny

PRINCIPLE: HOW I RESPOND TO LIFE'S STRUGGLES WILL DETERMINE MY DESTINY.

We can only see the value of our pain somewhere down the road. Are you willing to believe until then? My wife, Suzie's, first marriage had been to her high school sweetheart. After she became a Christian, she prayed for him to receive Jesus, but to no avail. Tragically, on the day he was going to file for divorce, he was killed flying a single engine plane.

Around midnight on the day of his fatal accident, her dad and mom came to break the news to her. Sobbing quietly, she went into her room to pack some clothes. A scripture on the wall above her bed caught her eye. It was a New Testament verse that would become pivotal, not just for Suzie's life, but for mine as well. Romans 8:28 says, "And we know that God causes everything to work together for the good of those who love God and are called according to His purpose for them." (NLT)

As the truth of this hope-filled scripture entered her heart, a calming peace gave her an inner confidence that God had everything under control. Within six months, she had joined our church planting team in Lake Tahoe and a short while later we fell in love.

Now, over three decades later, we have spent our lives giving hope to the hopeless; loving the seemingly unlovable, and watching God restore thousands of broken lives. Only by allowing God to heal us, can we realize our true destiny: helping others get healed in the same areas God has healed us. All of us will go through very challenging seasons. How we respond to these struggles will in some significant way determine our destiny. May we each rise to respond well.

1. **In what ways do you think your responses will shape your destiny?**

DAY

47

Jesus, Plus Nothing, Is Everything

PRINCIPLE: NOTHING BUT JESUS IS IMPORTANT. EVERYTHING COULD BE STRIPPED FROM MY LIFE AND I WILL STILL BE SUSTAINED.

Years ago, I went through a very challenging season when it seemed nothing was working out. All of my efforts were coming up empty. God's supernatural blessing, which at one point was evident in my life on a daily basis, was suddenly turned off. Doors were slamming shut and not reopening. I kept waiting for something to change. It wasn't a passing season; it was God making a solemn statement. He was rebooting my life.

One night, in the midst of my turmoil, I went on a sovereign prayer walk with God. I prayed from the deepest part of my being, "Jesus, even if lose everything, I can't lose You." It wasn't a cry of despair. It was a confident acknowledgment of God's unshakeable hand on my life. Deep inside, I knew nothing could separate me from God's love and care. My absolute conviction was, even if I lost everything else, His love for me would remain unshakeable.

This prayer was a major epiphany, spawning the life-changing revelation, Jesus, Plus Nothing, Is Everything. Nothing but Jesus is important; everything could be stripped from my life, and I will still be sustained. I was exhausted from trying to seethe my projects completed; this prayer of resignation produced a massive release of pressure. I didn't have to make things work out. My heart was being changed to enjoy the process of just knowing Him.

Today, don't pray for things to work out. It's a silly prayer, because none of us know what "things working out" looks like. Only God does. Pray to be satisfied with whatever Jesus provides for you. That satisfaction will demonstrate more than anything else that you trust Him. It's called "faith," and it alone will activate God's best for your life.

1 **What does the phrase, "Jesus, plus nothing, is everything" mean to you?**

DAY 48

The Secret of Satisfaction

PRINCIPLE: GOD DOESN'T GIVE ME WHAT I THINK I NEED, HE CHANGES MY HEART SO THAT I VALUE WHAT HE ALONE KNOWS I REALLY NEED.

What is the secret of a satisfied life? For years I have asked audiences, "Who here has not had a very difficult life? Please stand; we want to beat you up." Obviously, no hands were raised. It's true; life is hard. Yet, finding fulfillment in God is His will for each of us.

If anyone knew how to find satisfaction in life, it was the person God considered a man after His own heart, King David. David once wrote, "I shall be satisfied when I awake in Your likeness." (Psalms 17:15) David wasn't saying, "I'll be satisfied when all of my problems work out." Instead he responded out of the realization that God is the only One who will ever satisfy.

God's more concerned with the parts of our hearts that we haven't surrendered to Him than with the parts we have. Therefore, He doesn't give us what we think we need; God changes our hearts so that we value what He alone knows we really need.

So, how are we changed into God's likeness? Jesus tells us plainly, "Most assuredly, I say to you, unless a grain of wheat falls into the ground and dies, it remains alone; but if it dies, it produces much grain. He who loves his life will lose it, and he who hates his life in this world will keep it for eternal life." (John 12:24–25) The only way to find satisfaction in life is to die to our agenda and surrender to God's. It is in dying we live. God wants each of us to live our lives, and end our lives, satisfied. But He knows the only way for that to happen is for each of us to fully embrace His will.

1 Can you think of a situation in which God didn't give you what you thought you needed but later realized He gave you what you really needed?

DAY 49

What Are You Looking For?

PRINCIPLE: I DON'T NEED MORE THAN GOD DESIRES TO PROVIDE FOR ME.

When you wake up each morning, you need to decide what is most important to you. It will affect every aspect of your day. Paul wrote, "If then you were raised with Christ, seek those things which are above, where Christ is, sitting at the right hand of God. Set your mind [affections] on things above, not on things on the earth. For you died, and your life is hidden with Christ in God." (Colossians 3:1–2)

When I was a young Christian, I was driving with a seasoned missionary in an Asian nation. We had come to a stoplight where two lanes merged into one. In the next lane, revving his engine was a young guy in a brand new sports car. When the light turned green, much to my horror, the missionary floored the accelerator and cut off the sports car. All the while yelling, "No one gets ahead of the man of God!" I was speechless. I couldn't believe this man of God really thought being first was actually the goal in life. It may have been a momentary lapse or a chink in his armor, but either way, it was quite revealing.

In life, if we elbow our way to the front of the line, we will eventually come face to face with Christ's fine print, "But many who are first will be last, and the last first." (Matthew 19:30) I don't have to push my weight around. True promotion comes from God alone. (Psalms 75:6) He knows what I can and can't handle. I will entrust into His all-knowing hands my past, present, and future. I don't need more than He desires to provide for me. And with this fact of life, I will learn to be content in every situation. (Philippians 4:11–12, 1Timothy 6:6)

1 **What people/things are most important to you, and how do these affections influence your life?**

____

____

____

DAY

50 Why Are You Hanging Around Jesus?

PRINCIPLE: DYING TO SELF IS DESIGNED BY GOD TO BE ONE OF THE MOST EXHILARATING ADVENTURES IN LIFE.

Most people hung around Jesus for the loaves and the fishes—the proverbial hot meals. But His true disciples were completely committed even to the point of death. Trying to shake loose the sheep from the goats, Jesus once taught, "I assure you, unless you eat the flesh of the Son of Man and drink His blood, you cannot have eternal life within you." (John 6:53, NLT)

Jesus clearly did not make the bar as low as possible. The only relationship Jesus is willing have with anyone is a high-commitment relationship, the same kind a spouse requires. No spouse ever hoped his or her mate would be unfaithful. We each expect, even demand, 100 percent faithfulness. There are no allowances for affairs, not even on our birthdays. Jesus asks for no less commitment, no less devotion.

His disciples complained to each other, "This is very hard to understand. How can anyone accept it?" Yet Jesus knew that His disciples were confused, so He asked them, "Does this offend you?" (John 6:60–61, NLT) But His metaphor made the point. He was insistent: follow Me completely, or don't follow Me at all! "At this point many of His disciples turned away and deserted Him." (John 6:66, NLT) Yet, contrary to popular opinion, dying to self is not a miserable experience. It is designed by God to be one of the most exhilarating adventures in life.

1. How would you assess the Lord's commitment to you?
2. What is your current commitment to Him?

DAY

51 Dying Gracefully

PRINCIPLE: AS CHRISTIANS, WE SHOULD BE THE ONES WHO BEST KNOW HOW TO DIE.

A hundred years ago, a passenger ship sank while crossing the Atlantic Ocean. As it was going down, the occupants realized there were not enough lifeboats or lifejackets for everyone on board. Word spread quickly, soon coming to the attention of 109 Salvation Army officers. Consulting together, they made a courageous decision. They would each give their life jackets to others on board.

After the ship sank and the bodies of all 109 Salvation Army officers were found, not one of them had on a lifejacket. They had each drowned, willingly giving their lives for total strangers. Numerous reports of the officers' heroism were shared among the survivors. Over and over again, survivor's reported how the Salvation Army officers took off their own life jackets for others. Many of them, even women, persuading full-grown men to put on the jackets, pleading, "Take the jacket! I can die better than you can."

Could we make the same offer to those around us today? The struggle is that we all want a life jacket. Nobody wants to die. Yet, out of everyone on earth, we Christians should be the ones who best know how to die, dying daily to our own desires and wants. Is that how we view our own lives? Do we choose each day to die to our self? What would our friends and family say about us? There's no point in waiting for some grand moment to show our commitment, when every day we each have numerous opportunities to show what we are made of.

May we each receive the grace to demonstrate this level of Christ-likeness.

1. **Do you view your life as a daily choice to die to your own desires and wants?**
2. **In what ways do you reflect Christ-likeness to others?**

DAY 52

What's On God's Heart?

PRINCIPLE: THOSE WHO HAVE TRULY BEEN WASHED, HEALED, TOUCHED, AND REFRESHED IN GOD'S PRESENCE LEAVE THE COMFORTS OF HEAVEN AND JOIN HIM IN THE BATTLE FOR EARTH.

A friend of mine went into the wilderness to commune with God and frankly, to get away from people. While there, at a tender, broken moment in the middle of nowhere he prayed, "God, I'm always sharing what's on my heart. What's on Yours?" Just then he heard the sound of a small plane flying high overhead. Immediately, God's Spirit shot back, "The world—the world's on My heart!"

There seem to be many genuinely sincere Christians who are unwilling or unable to reach out to a lost and dying world. Some have spent their lives in mental speculation, tantalized by theological or eschatological possibilities. Yes, first love the Lord your God with all of your heart, mind, soul and strength; and out of that head-over-heels love relationship with God, we must love our neighbor as much as we love ourselves. Love should be the foundation of everything in our lives. Paul wrote, "If I gave everything I have to the poor and even sacrificed my body, I could boast about it; but if I didn't love others, I would be of no value whatsoever." (1Corinthians 13:3, NLT)

If the net effect of loving God is merely to muse on how much He loves us, then we have not heard His heart in His presence. The God who once loved the world still does. He continually invites those who have truly been washed, healed, touched and refreshed in His presence to leave the comforts of Heaven and join Him in the battle for Earth. Today, ask the Lord to show you someone on His heart. They are all around you.

1. **Is your heart in alignment with God's heart of love for others?**

DAY 53 What Were You Created For?

PRINCIPLE: REFUSE HATRED AND MISGUIDED INSULTS TO DESTROY YOUR INTIMACY WITH GOD.

As Oswald Chambers so eloquently said, "We are not made for brilliant moments, but we have to walk in the light of them in ordinary ways. There was only one brilliant moment in the life of Jesus, and that was on the Mount of Transfiguration; then He emptied Himself the second time of His glory, and came down into the demon-possessed valley. For 33years Jesus laid out His life to do the will of His Father..." (Oswald Chambers, *My Utmost For His Highest*, June 16th)

Jesus was dead long before He went to the cross. He was not dead physically, but dead to sin dead to His own will! If we really want to be like Jesus, we must first understand who He really was. He was a man of sorrows and acquainted with grief; despised and rejected, bruised, oppressed and afflicted. (Isaiah 53:3–5) Just like us, Jesus spent His whole life learning how to die to Himself and live for the Father and a lost and dying world.

The demon-possessed valley is calling us! It will not treat us well. We will not be appreciated, valued, and esteemed. These appropriate acknowledgements are for the distant future. The battle for now is not permitting the hatred on Earth to replace the love of Heaven. We must refuse to allow misguided insults to destroy our intimacy with God. We must fight to retain a kind and tender heart toward those wounded souls who have never tasted of the heavenly gift. All of the armies of Heaven are being deployed to assist us in this most noble of responses to the shortcomings of Earth.

1 In what ways do you fight to keep a kind and tender heart toward wounded people who don't know the Lord?

DAY

54 Dying Perfectly

PRINCIPLE: LEARNING TO DIE IS THE GREAT PREPARATION IN LIFE.

What will it take for us to learn to die?

Only one person ever perfectly modeled dying: the Lord Jesus Christ. In the Gospel of Mark, Jesus, nearing the end of His earthly ministry, came to the Garden of Gethsemane. Knowing the great battle He was about to face, "He said to His disciples, 'Sit here while I pray.' And He then took Peter, James, and John with Him, and began to be troubled and deeply distressed. Then Jesus said to them, 'My soul is exceedingly sorrowful, even to death. Stay here and watch.' " (Mark 14:32–34)

Jesus wasn't exaggerating the extent of His trouble, distress and sorrow! He was literally about to become the sin of the world. Consumed in grief, He felt like dying. This must have been the worst nightmare of His life. "He went a little farther, and fell on the ground, and prayed that if it were possible, the hour might pass from Him. And He said, 'Abba, Father, all things are possible for You. Take this cup away from Me; nevertheless, not what I will, but what You will.'" (Mark 14:35–36)

Jesus had spent His whole life disciplining His soul to die. Therefore, His response in the Garden of Gethsemane had three appropriate dimensions: complete faith, a willingness to forsake His own personal preference, and absolute trust.

First, Jesus had complete faith in the will of His Heavenly Father. He prayed unequivocally, "All things are possible for You." No solution was outside the reach of His Father in Heaven.

Secondly, Jesus expressed His human response to a heavenly dilemma, "Take this cup away from Me." What was this cup He preferred to not drink? The pain of crucifixion? Dying early in life? Leaving those He loved? I do not believe Jesus was unwilling to embrace any of the human challenges He faced. "Christ Jesus came into the world to save sinners." (1Timothy 1:15, NLT)

His challenge lay in eternity. When Jesus became sin for all humankind, at that moment His fellowship with His Father was broken. (2Corinthians 5:21) "God is light and in Him is no darkness at all." (1John 1:5) The God of light could, "have no fellowship with the unfruitful works of darkness." (Ephesians 5:11) On this side of eternity, we can have no idea how excruciatingly painful breaking fellowship with His Father was for the Lord Jesus Christ. Yet, without hesitation, Jesus was willing to temporarily lay aside His perfect bond with His Father in order to restore our relationship with God.

Summoning an inner strength, and resting on an absolute trust in God the Father, Jesus immediately yielded His will to the third and final appropriate response saying, "Nevertheless, not what I will, but what You will." What a perfect blend of faith and trust! What a perfect example for each of us!

Now, this is our time! This is our moment to model sublime death.

Live to die, and die to live!

1. **What experiences will it take for you to choose to die to yourself?**

2. **How strong is your trust in your heavenly Father that His will is always best?**

DAY 55

Living Beyond Personal Preference

PRINCIPLE: MY OVERPOWERING PREFERENCE IN LIFE IS TO FULLY EMBRACE GOD'S PREFERENCE.

How many preferences do you have in a day?

Would you believe preferences, like a drug, are addictive?

In the Book of Acts, Paul the Apostle faced the greatest challenge of his life: death by beheading. A prophetic word predicted going to Jerusalem meant danger, imprisonment and ultimately death. Paul likewise exhibited complete faith, a forsaking of his own personal preference, and absolute trust. He acknowledged, "And see, now I go bound in the spirit to Jerusalem, not knowing the things that will happen to me there, except that the Holy Spirit testifies in every city, saying that chains and tribulations await me." (Acts 20:22–23)

Paul refused to cower in fear at the likelihood of his suffering and death. Instead, he shot back, "But none of these things move me; nor do I count my life dear to myself, so that I may finish my race with joy, and the ministry which I received from the Lord Jesus, to testify to the gospel of the grace of God." (Acts 20:24) Paul again demonstrates complete faith and absolute trust in God. Is it any wonder Paul was chosen to write so much of the New Testament?

If we give into fear and personal preference, each of us will misinterpret the most important decisions of our lifetime. Likewise, if we are more concerned with preserving our lives, we will fail to fulfill God's perfect will for us. The breakthrough perspective each of us need most is, "Nothing is going to shake me!" You know you are dead when nothing can shake your dependence upon God. Sooner or later we each need to accept this fact: God is NOT trying to change our circumstances, He's trying to change our reaction to our circumstances.

I attempt to live every day beyond my addiction to having my own way. I consciously choose to trust the God I know, to fully discern the things I don't. He alone has all past, present and future understanding at His disposal, in order to make the decisions that are truly in my best interest. For only in eternity will I fully realize how God perfectly orchestrated every dimension of my life.

My overpowering preference in life is to fully embrace God's preference. In anticipation of this, every day, I wake up excited to see what He has picked out for me. Having had a natural father who planned few special things for my life, I now live continually in anticipation of the magnificent surprises my heavenly Father has prepared for me. "No eye has seen, no ear has heard, and no mind has imagined what God has prepared for those who love Him. But we know these things because God has revealed them to us by His Spirit...." (1Corinthians 2:9–10, NLT)

Reveal them to us today, Oh God! We expectantly await Your surprises!

1 How many preferences do you experience daily?

2 In what ways do these preferences affect your life?

DAY 56

Dodging Death and Living Life

PRINCIPLE: EACH OF US WERE CREATED FOR ONE SHINING MOMENT. PREPARE FOR IT.

Do you see the value of the most mundane dimensions in your life?

I knew a woman who was driving with her boyfriend in an open jeep. They were off-road, driving up a mountain in the Rockies, outside of Denver, Colorado. Her two daughters, five and seven years old, were both seat-belted in the back of the jeep.

As the boyfriend parked the vehicle on the side of a steep hill, he failed to set the brake properly. Moments after walking away, the jeep began to roll backwards down the hill, tumbling over and over while careening toward a cliff. Amazingly, because of their seatbelts, the girls were not thrown out.

The only thing that could keep the vehicle and the girls from launching over the cliff was one straggly tree perched at the edge of the precipice. If the jeep did not hit the tree perfectly, or if the tree failed to stop the jeep on impact, then the jeep and the two little girls would plummet over the cliff, falling to their death. But as God would have it, the tree caught the jeep, saving the girls' lives. Though the vehicle was totaled, the daughters walked away without a scratch.

I've thought a lot about that tree over the years. Many people would have considered the tree useless; sitting in the middle of nowhere, doing absolutely nothing of consequence. But God had a different plan. In His infinite wisdom He knew, "I'll make this tree, that no one will think has value, for one shining moment—to save two little girls."

I can also imagine as the tree sized up the situation, it braced for its big opportunity. At first, it had been spacing out in the afternoon sun, but seeing the jeep hurdling toward it, adrenalin shot through its trunk. Digging its roots in, bracing for impact, the tree gave everything it had to absorb the collision of the jeep; and much to its delight the children were spared.

That night, after the jubilant family had gone home, with the jeep permanently lodged in its wounded side, the bruised and battered tree probably called out to a friend on a nearby mountaintop, "Hey Aspen, did you see that today? You know how I'm always complaining about nothing significant ever happening to me? Well, today was different! This was the greatest day of my life! Today, I rescued two little girls from certain death. It made all those boring, lonely years worth living. For the rest of my life, I'll probably never have another opportunity like this, so I'll cherish this day forever."

Each of us at some point in our lives will find ourselves plummeting toward a cliff and certain death. In that moment, the only thing separating us from an eternity estranged from our loving Creator will be one straggly tree: the cross of Jesus. From the beginning of time that lone tree was in the heart of the Father, created for one purpose: to sacrifice His only Son for the sins of the world. If we miss that tree, our fate is sealed. If we embrace it, we will be eternally grateful that God spared our lives.

1. **Are you able to see the value in the most mundane aspects of your life?**

2. **Have you ever experienced God using one of these aspects of your life to impact another person?**

DAY 57 Free Love Bankrupted Me

PRINCIPLE: THE SEED FOR AN AUTHENTIC RELATIONSHIP WITH MY CREATOR HAS BEEN FIRMLY PLANTED IN MY SPIRIT.

Being a charter member in the free love movement cost so much, I'm still making payments. For years I tried to make love a god when, in truth, only God is love. It was not until I found Jesus at 23 that I realized each of my many imperfections had been marvelously covered by God's matchless love and perfection. I needed a Savior. He wanted a son. We were made for each other. Actually, I was made for Him.

For me, after my salvation, God's presence in those early days permeated our every waking moment. We were in love. We sang, laughed, and cried for joy. We wanted everyone in the world to know our Jesus and set out to tell anyone who would listen. Though my longing for purpose was greatly satisfied when I was born again, my heart yearned to be fully immersed in a community of authentic people. My hope in knowing Jesus was that honesty with others would bring the complete overhaul I desperately needed. Initially it did, but the price for being fully transparent was difficult to maintain.

Over time, my abject abandon turned into cautious commitment. The mantra, "I'll do anything for you, Jesus" morphed into "Now God, what exactly did You have in mind?" My willingness to do "whatever… for whomever…whenever" evolved into doing "somewhat… for some…sometimes." But the seed for an authentic relationship with my Creator had been firmly planted in my spirit.

No substitute would do. It is the same today. I yearn for the authentic—longing for first love once again. Jesus, come today. Sweep me off my feet. Let me soar with You above the mediocrity of Earth.

1 **How would you assess your current relationship with God- abject abandon or cautious commitment?**

DAY 58 Breaking the Silence

PRINCIPLE: THE DOORWAY INTO ACCEPTANCE AND LOVE IS FULL DISCLOSURE.

Do we share honestly and openly what is going on inside of us?

Or do we hide?

Jesus held back nothing His Father had given Him. He transparently made known His thoughts and broke the silence between God and man; between God and friends; even between God and enemies. No wonder His disciples were willing to give their lives for Him. His naked vulnerability, not just on the cross of Calvary, but throughout their three and a half years with Him, affirmed His continual commitment to share His entire being with those He loved.

The sin of Judas was doubly hurtful when we realize Jesus had created an unparalleled atmosphere of openness and honesty amongst His disciples. He shared His heart, and each of His wounded followers had complete liberty to share as well. If someone sinned, all he had to do was admit his error and he would have been forgiven. No one suspected Judas would breach this trust and betray Jesus.

It was unthinkable to imagine that this highly respected disciple would refuse this once-in-a-lifetime opportunity for full disclosure—this miraculous doorway into full acceptance and love. It was so unnecessary; so incomprehensibly shallow. All he had to say was, "I've been living a double life: stealing from our funds and harboring real bitterness toward you, Jesus. I am so sorry!" But, instead, he kept silent and allowed the cancer in his heart to contaminate his whole life, and destroy his destiny. Jesus disclosed this horrifying truth, "...how terrible it will be for my betrayer. Far better for him if he had never been born!" (Mark 14:21, NLT)

How many of us share our inner struggles and victories with others? Do we live such honest, open, and transparent lives for Jesus Christ that we are truly living epistles, "known and read by all men?" (2Corinthians 3:2)

Are we, as born again Christians, willing to die to ourselves in order to break the silence of fear, doubt and unbelief; testifying of the marvelous victories God has accomplished in our lives and, even more importantly, our struggles?

The cry of the psalmists echoes through the corridors of Heaven, "Let the redeemed of the Lord say so, Whom He has redeemed from the hand of the enemy." (Psalms 107:2)

It's time to speak!

It's time to break the silence!

1 **Do you regularly share transparently with others?**

2 **In what ways has your transparency affected you and others?**

DAY 59 Overcoming The Devil

PRINCIPLE: THE KEY TO OVERCOMING THE DEVIL IS IN MY HEART AND MOUTH.

The primary purpose of Jesus is ours as well. For one principle reason, with many marvelous overtones: "For this purpose the Son of God was manifested, that He might destroy the works of the devil." (1John 3:8b) The devil, once named Lucifer, the morning star, is now known as Satan, the archenemy of good. In eternity past, known as the anointed cherub and worship leader of Heaven, he has been temporarily thrust down to the Earth awaiting his eventual doom and eternal torment. (Revelation 20:10)

The Bible clearly asserts there are only three possible ways to overcome the temptations of Satan: " they overcame [the devil] by the blood of the Lamb, and by the word of their testimony, and they did not love their lives to the death." (Revelation 12:11)

The word "testimony" means evidence given, a record or report. It refers to the record or report of what Jesus Christ has accomplished in rescuing our lives. The words testimony and martyr are derived from the same root word.

Only by embracing all that the shed blood of Jesus accomplished can each of us receive a testimony worth dying for. But too many Christians, after being joyfully born into a relationship with Jesus Christ, choose to remain silent, both about their struggles and the astounding blessings we have been given as sons and daughters of God. The silence must be broken, or the very rocks will scream out what God has done. (Luke 19:40)

1. **What is the best way you can overcome the devil?**
2. **Are you willing to regularly share your testimony with those who don't know Jesus?**

DAY 60 Naked, But Not Ashamed

PRINCIPLE: THE GREAT JOY IN LIFE IS BEING ABLE TO SAY, "SATAN HAS NOTHING IN ME."

All babies have two things in common; they are born clueless and clothes-less.

The idea that God is somehow squeamish about humans being naked is laughable. Whatever we've got, He's seen. But does this universal reality have an even greater significance in the spirit realm? Let's go back to the first bodies. The first human beings, Adam and Eve, were quite happy running around naked. Genesis 2:25 reads, "And they were both naked [to be or to make bare], the man and his wife, and were not ashamed [disappointed or confused]."

God isn't a prude, Eve didn't blush, and Adam felt zero guilt when he looked at his naked wife. In a sinless, untainted world, nakedness was seen as the norm; viewed without a shred of shame, embarrassment or guilt. Was this atmosphere of, shall we say, full disclosure, limited to the physical dimension? Not at all! The original man and woman were completely open with God and one another. Candor and honesty ruled, until deception and deceit attempted to overthrow the Kingdom of God.

Satan, appropriately titled the "father of lies," (John 8:44) intentionally seduced our fore-parents. Today, the seduction continues. Fully imbedded within the surface morality of our culture, the devil offers godlikeness, devoid of God.

Situational ethics, intertwined with man-centered morality is the subplot behind much of today's music, movies and media. Our culture is a shell of what God intended.

So, is nakedness a good thing? Absolutely! In two specific situations: physically, between a husband and a wife; and metaphorically, in every healthy relationship available to man. As in the beginning, God wants us to be naked and transparent with Him; "And there is no creature hidden from His sight, but all things are naked and open to the eyes of Him to whom we must give account." (Hebrews 4:13, NKJV)

Jesus affirmed this essential principle of transparency when He said, "No one, when he has lit a lamp, puts it in a secret place or under a basket, but on a lamp stand, that those who come in may see the light. The lamp of the body is the eye. Therefore, when your eye is good [clear, properly folded together], your whole body also is full of light [lustrous, bright, transparent or well-illuminated]. But when your eye is bad [hurtful], your body also is full of darkness [opaque or impervious to light, so that images cannot be seen through it]." (Luke 11:33–34, NKJV)

Here's a paraphrase of these two verses, "When your vision is clear, then your life will be in order, fully transparent, bright and illuminated for others to see. But when your vision is blurred by hurt, then your life is opaque, impervious to light, so that others cannot see the person God intended you to be."

Perhaps, when Jesus said, "Satan has 'nothing in Me' " (John 14:30, NKJV) He was implying, "There is nothing Satan can use against me because nothing is hidden." Jesus was saying. "What you see is what you get! My life is transparent, wide open for everyone, including My Heavenly Father to see!"

1 Is your life transparent for others to see? Why?

2 How would you living openly before others bless your life?

DAY 61 Living Love

PRINCIPLE: I AM BEING DRAWN INTO A COMMUNITY OF EVER-DEEPENING RELATIONSHIPS, WHERE EVERYONE IS NOT JUST LISTENED TO, BUT HEARD.

Though everyone in our culture is talking about love, few are experiencing the real deal. More often than not, what is called love is the counterfeit, sugarcoated, eye-candy variety whose satisfaction rate can be measured in seconds. Yet real love still beckons, offering each of us an immeasurable return on our heart-felt investment.

A Gallup survey found six basic inner needs throughout society. They are:

1. To believe that life is meaningful and has a purpose.
2. For a sense of community and deeper relationships.
3. To be listened to and to be heard.
4. To feel that one is growing in faith.
5. To be appreciated and respected.
6. For practical help in developing a mature faith.

Genuine Christians, transparent and caring, have the grace and God-given capacity to live the life described in the Gallup survey. We as Christians have found the meaning and purpose of life. We have been called to be a loving fellowship where each person can feel they are growing in faith; and where all are appreciated and respected as they mature in faith and love by knowing and living for Jesus.

Today, listen to someone—really listen to their heart, not just their words. Find someone needing God's unconditional love and share it freely with them. Expect nothing in return. The reward is in the giving.

Before you leave the planet, develop a reputation as someone who loves God whole-heartedly, loves others selflessly, and was willing to take risks in both areas. Living Love—what a gift!

1 In what ways do you live out authentic love?

DAY 62

Identification vs. Persuasion

PRINCIPLE: WITHOUT IDENTIFICATION THERE IS NO PERSUASION.

Do people identify with our lives? If they don't, our words can't make up for the miscommunication. Can they see our struggles and victories, and what it means to be a genuine Christ follower in a disingenuous age? Not just our emotional highs, but our emotional lows. Not just our feeling-filled lows, but our faith-filled highs.

The profound impact of identification can be seen in the Book of Ruth. Ruth pledged solidarity with her mother-in-law, Naomi: "For wherever you go, I will go; and wherever you lodge, I will lodge; your people shall be my people, and your God, my God." (Ruth 1:16b) That was identification; and without identification there is no persuasion. Unless people hear a broken tenderness in your voice, don't expect to hear it in theirs. Unless they see a caring gleam in our eye, we will reap exactly what we have sown.

Jesus was the most authentic, genuine person who ever walked the face of the earth. If we have any hope of representing Him effectively on this earth, our lives must in some way model that same level of humble integrity as well. Christ in you, your only hope of glorifying God. (Colossians 1:27)

I love the way Tim Keel sums up this point: "It's easy to be a preacher; all you have to do is stand in front of your people and open your vein. But that requires discernment and vulnerability."

Today, open a vein. Pour out the life-blood of a love that is irresistible. It's what Jesus did. It's what He wants to do through us as His representatives.

Jesus hasn't left the Earth. He's still here, if we want Him to be.

1. **Do you share your struggles and victories with others?**
2. **As others identify with you, how do you share Jesus with them?**

DAY 63

From Sick-of-Love to Lovesick

PRINCIPLE: THERE'S A BIG DIFFERENCE BETWEEN KNOWING THE GOD OF LOVE, AND KNOWING THE GOD WHO IS IN LOVE.

When I first gave my heart to Jesus, I was so burned out on my attempts to find true love, that I remained celibate for three years until my marriage to Suzie—no dating, no flirting, just Jesus. The selfless love He freely offered was so refreshing to my wary soul, it immediately replaced the self-centered love to which I had been accustomed. I was learning about a whole new kind of love; where "in lowliness of mind… each esteem[s] others [as] better than himself." (Philippians 2:3) I was soon to realize that everything God does is designed to lead us into intimacy with Him.

Old Testament marriages were often business arrangements that parents made for their children. So the soon-to-be husband and wife didn't like each other? No problem. They would learn to work things out.

But Solomon and his Shulammite bride were a different story. They wrote the book on romance. The account in Song of Solomon of the impassioned love between a husband and wife matches the relationship Jesus longs for with His Church. In desperation the bride says, "I looked for him but did not find him. I will get up now and go about the city, through its streets and squares; I will search for the one my heart loves... When I found the one my heart loves…I held him and would not let him go." (Song of Solomon 3:1–2, 4, NIV)

Why are we not "lovesick" (Song of Solomon 5:8) when we stray away from our Lord? Is it because He doesn't love us enough? Nothing could be further from the truth. The groom says, "Sixty queens there may be, and eighty concubines, and virgins beyond number; but my dove, my perfect one, is unique." (Song of Solomon 6:8–9, NIV) Amazing but true, that is each one of us, seen from God's perspective.

We can never know God's love until we fail and then realize He is still madly in love with us. As Mike Bickle so often says, "God is not just a God of love, He is a God in love." He has never held back in sharing His impassioned love for us.

Likewise, we should not refrain from continuously giving our heartfelt love to Him. At times our love will be expressed in an honest heart of worship; at other times it will be demonstrated in a vulnerable testimony of God's saving grace.

At all times, let God's love be fully received—let it be fully revealed in us and through us.

1. **Have you fully embraced the God who is in love with you?**
2. **How do you express your love for Him?**

DAY
64 A Death Defying Leap

PRINCIPLE: IF I CAN LEARN TO LIVE IN THE LIGHT, I WILL NEVER HAVE TO FEAR THE DARKNESS.

The cross of Jesus is alive and working!

In 1967, Charles Murray was training as a high diver for the '68 Summer Olympics. During that season of his life, a Christian friend regularly talked with him about his need for a personal relationship with Jesus Christ. Though Charles insisted he was not ready to give his life to Jesus, one day he called his friend and wanted to know where to look in the New Testament for some verses about salvation.

Late that same night, Charles decided to go to the pool and practice his diving. His Olympic status gave him special privileges to use the University pool even during off hours. The pool area had a ceiling of glass panels, and on this particular night a full moon illuminated the pool sufficiently for him to dive by moonlight.

Enjoying the atmosphere, Charles climbed to the highest platform in the darkness to make his first dive. As he did, the Spirit of God began to convict him of his sin. All of the Scriptures he had read that day began to flood his mind. Going to the edge of the platform, he turned around and faced the wall, preparing to dive backwards

Spreading his arms to gather his balance, Charles gazed at the wall. He was stunned by what he saw; the light of the moon caused the silhouette of his outstretched arms to form the shape of a cross. Instantly, Charles was overcome by his sin. His heart was so broken by the convicting power of the Spirit he immediately sat down on the platform and prayerfully asked Jesus to forgive him and save him.

Suddenly, the lights came on. An attendant had come in to check the pool area. As Charles looked over at him, he happened to look down into the pool. To his shock and horror, he realized the pool had been emptied of all its water. It had been drained that day for repairs. God had saved his life that day in more ways than one. Charles had nearly jumped to his death, but the cross had spared him. His miraculous rescue affirms what Paul wrote in his letter to the Corinthians, “For the message of the cross is foolishness to those who are perishing, but to us who are being saved it is the power of God.” (1Corinthians 1:18)

May we each one day kneel in humility before our faithful Creator and surrender to His will for our lives. Only then will we have the potential to live the fully transparent, bright and illuminated lives God intended for us. “This is the message which we have heard from Him and declare to you, that God is light and in Him is no darkness at all. If we say that we have fellowship with Him, and walk in darkness, we lie and do not practice the truth. But if we walk in the light as He is in the light, we have fellowship with one another, and the blood of Jesus Christ His Son cleanses us from all sin.” (1John 1:5–7) Giving in to darkness will eventually kill us. In contrast, only by surrendering to Jesus Christ, the true Light of the world, can we be saved. (John1:9)

If we can learn to live in the light, we will never have to fear the darkness.

1. **What did your life look like when you were walking in darkness?**

2. **How is your life different now that you're walking with Jesus in the light?**

DAY 65 Clarity Is Overrated

PRINCIPLE: TRUST IS BELIEVING THAT GOD HAS ALL THE CLARITY I NEED FOR EVERY SITUATION IN MY LIFE.

A man visited the House of the Dying in Calcutta, India, for three months, to find out how to best spend the rest of his life. When he met Mother Teresa she asked, "What can I do for you?" He asked her to pray for him.

"What do you want me to pray for?" she responded. He then shared the most pressing burden on his heart, "Pray that I may have clarity."

Mother Teresa responded firmly, "No, I will not do that." Surprised, he asked her why. She told him, "Clarity is the last thing you are clinging to and must let go of."

"But," he told her, "you always seem to have the clarity I long for." She laughed and said, "I have never had clarity; what I have always had is trust. So I will pray that you trust God."

Trust is believing that God has all the clarity we need for every situation in our lives. I don't need to know what's going on. Often, my assumptions about life are really presumptions. I'm not wallowing in ignorance, I'm resting in confident trust.

When I was growing up on car trips with my parents, like all kids, I would periodically ask, "When will we get there?" A valid question, though when repeated every other minute, it can be annoying. But, I never asked my parents "Do you know where we are going?" I assumed they knew. I trusted they knew. I rested in their knowing.

At times God shares this clarity with us, and on other occasions He withholds it for a more suitable time.

1. What do you usually depend on for peace, clarity, or trust in God?

2. If you trusted God more, how would it affect your life?

DAY 66 Total Trust

PRINCIPLE: THE MORE I KNOW GOD THE MORE I TRUST HIM.

Do you trust God completely? It will be demonstrated by how relaxed you are in your soul and spirit when you're in the big fat middle of a storm.

The reason we do not trust God is because we do not know Him. Just as you can only trust someone you know, the reverse is also true; you cannot know someone unless you first trust him. If we know God we would certainly love and trust Him; and that means trusting Him to reveal His understanding to us, in His timing, not ours. The trusting person is the one who is no more attached to God giving him clarity than God staying silent. It makes no difference. He knows the main event is not "me knowing what's going on." The supreme need-to-know in life is that "God knows what's going on."

Most people traveling on commercial airplanes never ask the pilot what he is doing. Instead, we trust that the person in the cockpit is fully competent to handle any and all emergencies. If the weather rattles us a bit, we still believe the plane will remain intact, and the pilot will guide us safely home. The track record of the airline only adds to our confidence; an impeccable safety record further enhances trust. It is the same way with God. Speaking through the psalmist, the Spirit of God issues an eternal promise; "Once I was young, and now I am old. Yet I have never seen the godly forsaken…" (Psalms 37:25a, NLT)

The more we know God the more we trust Him.

The more we depend upon our own understanding, the less peace we have, and the less enjoyable life we live. (Proverbs 3:5–6)

Trust God and enjoy your life!

1. **As you know God more, is your trust in Him growing?**
2. **How does it affect you when you put your complete trust in Him?**

DAY 67

What Are You Attached To?

PRINCIPLE: I DON'T NEED TO FIGURE OUT WHAT'S GOING ON AS LONG AS I TRUST THE GOD WHO ALREADY KNOWS.

Are you more attached to knowing God, or receiving His blessing? Your focus will completely affect the outcome.

More than anyone else in our lives, God wants to continually commune with us. Moses and Joshua understood this. "So the Lord spoke to Moses face to face, as a man speaks to his friend." (Exodus 33:11a) Real trust is no longer being dependent upon God's blessing, but upon being desperate to know God Himself. Blessings can be misinterpreted, whereas our trust in someone we know remains unshakeable.

1Peter 1:7 in the King James Version of the Bible refers to "...the trial of your faith, being much more precious than of gold..." The word trial here implies trustworthiness. The trials of life reveal our trust in God, and therefore are the most valuable lesson we can learn in life. Until we esteem the promises in God's Word above our own thoughts, we will continue to chafe whenever something goes contrary to our expectations. Have you noticed, that things going contrary to your expectations every day?

God provides a reality check of who He is in the Book of Isaiah, "For My thoughts are not your thoughts, nor are your ways My ways," says the Lord. (Isaiah 55:8) I don't need to figure out what's going on as long as I trust the God who already knows.

The next time you think God is withholding insight from you, believe that it would be way too much information. "No good thing will the LORD withhold from those who do what is right." (Psalms 84:11b)

1. **What lessons have you learned about your trust in God from the trials in your life?**

DAY 68

Mother Teresa's Perspective

PRINCIPLE: I'LL ONLY BE ABLE TO SEE GOD WORKING IN MY LIFE WHEN I CAN SEE MY LIFE FROM GOD'S PERSPECTIVE.

What made Mother Teresa's life so different?

Because Mother Teresa loved the life God gave her, she was able to love the people God sent her. Less than five feet tall and slightly more than 100 pounds, this giant of a woman fully accepted everyone and everything God sent her way. She embraced the outrageous circumstances she encountered, turning impossible situations into divine appointments. She saw God in her circumstances because she was willing see her life from God's point of view.

In a video about her life, Mother Teresa looked confidently into the camera and said, "...be where He wants you to be. If He puts you in the street, if everything is taken from you and suddenly you find yourself in the street, to accept to be in the street at that moment. Not for you to put yourself in the street, but to accept to be put there. To accept if God wants you to be in a palace, well then to accept to be in the palace as long as you are not choosing to be in the palace."

She continued "This is what makes the difference in total surrender; to accept whatever He gives, and to give whatever it takes with a big smile. This is the surrender to God; to accept to be cut to pieces and yet every piece to belong only to Him. This is the surrender. To accept all the people that come, the work that you happen to do. Today, maybe you have a good meal and tomorrow maybe you have nothing. To accept and to give whatever it takes. If it takes your good name, if it takes your good health, that's the surrender. That is it! You are free then!"

1. **What most impacts you about the way Mother Teresa chose to live?**

2. **How does it affect you when you begin to see a situation in light of God's perspective?**

DAY 69

Momentary Light Afflictions

PRINCIPLE: INSTEAD OF SINKING ME, THE PRESSURES IN MY LIFE ACTUALLY ANCHOR ME TO THE ONE WHO LOVES ME MOST.

Have you lost heart? God knows where it is. He will help you find it.

Earth is short; Heaven is long, and what happens here doesn't stay here. We will either take it with us as an eternal reward or an everlasting regret. Our time here is actually the shortest chapter of our endless lives, but it is also the one that will set the tone for eternity. While it is appropriate to rejoice in its brevity, it is wise to be concerned with its finality.

Let the Apostle Paul's words lift your spirits, "Therefore we do not lose heart. Even though our outward man is perishing, yet the inward man is being renewed day by day. For our light affliction [pressure, anguish, burdens, trouble], which is but for a moment, is working for us a far more exceeding and eternal weight of glory…" (2Corinthians 4:16–17) The eternal glory that will be revealed in our lives will be worth every pressure and burden we have gone through.

The challenge comes, not in that we have pressures, but in how we view them. If they are anchors around our necks weighing us down in despair, then we are missing their point entirely. Instead of sinking us, the pressures in our lives actually anchor us to the One who loves us most.

In eternity, we will thank God for each trial He so wisely designed with us in mind. There are no accidental struggles in life; just marvelously crafted stretching's that not only bring out the best in us, but, once ours eyes are opened, reveal the best of God's all-wise intentions for us.

1. **Have you had a time in your life where you became hopeless and lost heart?**
2. **How did this experience anchor you more to the love of God?**

DAY 70 When Concerns Are Not Yours

PRINCIPLE: I SHOULD ONLY BE AS CONCERNED ABOUT MY FUTURE AS GOD IS.

Just as beauty is in the eyes of the beholder, bondage is as well. I have a choice in how I see my life. No one, and no situation can force me to be depressed or discouraged, angry or bitter. These deformed responses to life are all in my court. I can welcome them as friends, or dismiss them as the distracting enemies they are.

Most of the time, I choose to see my life from God's point of view. "Now thanks be to God who always leads us in triumph in Christ, and through us diffuses the fragrance of His knowledge in every place." (2Corinthians 2:14,) I was made to triumph with Him always and forever. Every situation in my life is an opportunity to see the miraculous, saving hand of God. I can live with excited anticipation of how God is going to deliver me out of my seeming predicaments, or I can wait fretting when the proverbial other shoe will fall. This is one situation where I am decidedly "pro-choice." I choose to see my life from God's point of view. He is not concerned about the adventure He has prepared for me, nor should I be.

We are what we think. If we think we are afraid, then so we are. Proverbs says it so clearly. "For as he thinks in his heart, so is he." (Proverbs 23:7) I need to think God's thoughts, not my own. I need the mind of Christ, not the mind of Francis. I must learn to cast my burden on the Lord and let Him sustain me. (Psalms 55:22) We should only be as concerned about our future as God is.

1. **What is currently most concerning to you?**
2. **What do you think would happen if you daily chose to view this situation as an unfinished work of God?**

DAY 71 Daunting Difficulties

PRINCIPLE: MY GOAL EACH DAY IS TO NOT LET EVEN ONE DROP OF ANXIETY TOUCH MY HEART AND MIND.

Which is bigger—God or your problems?

One of history's men of faith experienced firsthand the saving grace of God in extraordinarily challenging situations. "...king [David]...said, 'As the Lord lives, [He] has redeemed my life from every distress...' " (1Kings 1:29) Likewise, in the Book of Samuel, he again reiterates this same unshakeable conviction, "... David answered...them, 'As the Lord lives, [He] has redeemed my life from all adversity...'" (2Samuel 4:9)

The difficulties David faced were daunting and overwhelming, traversing his entire life. Here is but a sampling: David accepted and defeated the intimidating challenge of the giant Goliath; (1Samuel 17) he pretended to be insane in front of King Achish; (1Samuel 21) he hid in the caves of Adullam from King Saul, (1Samuel 22–23) and when his son Absalom wanted to overthrow him and have him killed, (2Samuel 15:10–13) David placed his trust in the living God.

Over and over again, David was delivered from one impossible situation after another. He knew how temporary and light every affliction really was. No trial would alter his unshakeable conviction.

Once, when I was preaching on this subject, halfway through my message, I took off my outer shirt to reveal a T-shirt that, in giant letters, read, "I have no problems!" I know it shocked and perhaps irritated some people in the meeting who thought I was crazy. Was I living in denial or deception? I then told the audience, "I'm living a stress-free life; a pressure-free existence, snuggled in the hollow of God's hand. What I have is not only possible; it's essential for each of you. I invite you to join me."

I then turned away from the audience and displayed the backside of my shirt that read, "God's got a lot of problems and I'm praying for Him." The audience laughed at this tongue-in-cheek expression, but they understood my point. If I am truly "casting all of my cares upon the One who cares most for me," (1Peter 5:7) then why am I not living the carefree life? If I am indeed challenged by Scripture to be "anxious for nothing," (Philippians 4:6) then my goal is to not let even one drop of anxiety touch my heart and mind.

1. **What are you anxious about and why do you think it's merited?**

2. **Read Philippians 4:6 as a command and not a suggestion. How will you obey today?**

DAY 72 If Only...

PRINCIPLE: LEARN TO LOOK PAST YOUR SETBACKS AND YOU WILL DISCOVER THE PURPOSE IN YOUR PAIN.

Have you ever looked back on a situation in your life in which you wish you could get a "Do Over"? I have, many times.

Growing up, my twin brother and I had a very competitive relationship. What one of us could do, the other was determined to do better! Once, in my early teens, my brother dared me to go down a steep hill on my bike without using any brakes and make a 90-degree turn into our driveway. After watching him successfully maneuver the seemingly impossible feat (I found out later he was braking with his hidden right hand), it was my turn.

There I went, screaming down the hill. By the time I reached the driveway, I quickly realized I had absolutely no chance of making the turn, and so I did the only thing I could do—I froze. My bicycle then hit a one-foot-high wall separating our neighbor's driveway from our own at 300 mph. Together, my bike and I did a complete somersault in the air, sailing over the adjacent driveway and finally landed in a large pile of jagged rocks.

Lying bloodied and bruised, I glanced over to see my brother Joseph sprawled out on our front yard, roaring with laughter. He said it was the funniest thing he had ever seen: me upside-down on my bike with a look of sheer terror etched on my face. Our motto back then was, "It's not funny until someone gets hurt, and then it's hilarious." When my brother realized how serious my injuries were, he did become more sensitive, accompanying my mother and me to the hospital. Fifteen stitches, and several decades later, I now laugh about the prank, but back then I wanted an immediate do-over. That, of course, was impossible.

Like myself, many people suffer from an acute case of the "if onlys." If only I were smarter; had more money; were prettier; had a different body; could lose weight; could get married; wasn't married; had a baby; didn't have children; had a different job; had a job; hadn't made that mistake; had a best friend; could go back in time; married a different person; or were raised differently.

If only God would do this one thing for me. If only, if only, if only…

Our lives are not a waste of time; everything we go through has value! God perfects us through our difficulties. “So even though Jesus was God’s Son, He learned obedience from the things He suffered.” (Hebrews 5:8, NLT)

Difficulties don’t produce character; they reveal it.

There is purpose in every setback. In Matthew 26:31–32, Jesus was aware that His sudden arrest and crucifixion would wreak havoc on His disciples. Therefore He told them, “All of you will be made to stumble because of Me this night, for it is written: ‘I will strike the Shepherd, and the sheep of the flock will be scattered.’ But after I have been raised, I will go before you to Galilee.”

Learn to look past your setbacks and you will discover the purpose in your pain. If you are focusing on your pain, you are still living in the past. No good can come from watering last year’s crop. The ancient philosopher Euripides once wrote, “Waste not fresh tears over old griefs.”

1 How have your setbacks motivated your passion and purpose?

DAY

73 Indispensable Pain

PRINCIPLE: THERE ARE TIMES WHEN ONLY OUR PERSONAL PAIN CAN HUMBLE AND PROTECT US.

Ashlyn Blocker is fearless, say her parents and kindergarten teachers. But her fearlessness is not courage based; it's because she can't feel pain. When she eats at the school cafeteria, teachers have to put ice in her chili so she doesn't burn her mouth. Five-year-old Ashlyn would never know until the damage was done and she had swallowed the chili scalding hot.

Over the few short years of her life, Ashlyn has chewed through her tongue while eating, and torn the flesh off her finger, not realizing how she was hurting herself.

Only a few people have ever been diagnosed with what Ashlyn has—anhidrosis, or CIPA—a rare genetic disorder giving her a congenital insensitivity to pain.

Looking at photos of Ashlyn over the years you can trace the history of self-inflicted injuries. One of the pictures shows her in a Christmas dress, hair beautifully fixed, with a swollen lip, missing tooth, and puffy eye. With her hands wrapped in athletic tape to protect them, she smiles gleefully like a boxer who just won a prizefight.

Ashlyn's mother, Tara Blocker, provides further understanding for all of us as to why pain is so essential for life, "Pain's there for a reason. It lets your body know something's wrong and it needs to be fixed. I'd give anything for her to feel pain."

Why do we resist the gift of pain? Why do we second guess the perfect plans of an omniscient Creator? Our shallow understanding merely consigns us to miss the point of purposeful circumstances, needlessly repeating the learning process tailor-made for each of our precious lives.

The inability to feel pain is not new. For thousands of years lepers have reaped the tragic fruit of life without the sensation of pain. Leprosy is a chronic infectious disease, which attacks the skin. Cuts and bruises are not felt, and often get infected because the person is unaware he is hurt. Each year more than two million people worldwide are diagnosed with this sensory loss, which left untreated will cause parts of the body to become deformed or even die. Throughout history lepers have been rejected outcasts, isolated in colonies where they often died with little or no treatment and care.

Many times in life we naively pray, "Lord, if I just didn't have to experience so much pain, my life would be great." In truth, it is the pain of life that keeps us humble, increases our dependence upon God and others, and causes us to reconsider foolish actions that can damage and destroy our lives. Pain protects us.

Malcolm Muggeridge, the famous British journalist and author, wrote near the end of his life, "Contrary to what might be expected, I look back on experiences that at the time seemed especially desolating and painful with particular satisfaction. Indeed, I can say with complete truthfulness that everything I have learned in my 75 years in this world, everything that has truly enhanced and enlightened my experience, has been through affliction and not through happiness." (Malcolm Muggeridge, in Homemade, July, 1990)

1 In what ways has pain humbled and protected you?

2 How has your pain increased your dependence on God and others?

DAY

74 Surf's Up

PRINCIPLE: MAJESTIC JOY EMERGES FROM THE GREATEST STRUGGLES.

Oswald Chambers in his classic devotional, *My Utmost For His Highest*, wrote, "Huge waves that would frighten an ordinary swimmer produce a tremendous thrill for the surfer who has ridden them. Let's apply that to our own circumstances. The things we try to avoid and fight against—tribulation, suffering, and persecution—are the very things that produce abundant joy in us. 'In all these things we are more than conquerors through Him who loved us.' (Romans 8:37) In all these things, not in spite of them, but in the midst of them. A saint doesn't know the joy of the Lord in spite of tribulation, but because of it. Paul said, "I am exceedingly joyful in all our tribulation." (2Corinthians 7:4) Enjoying life means we are living 'in joy' and not 'in confusion or frustration.' (Oswald Chambers, *My Utmost For His Highest*, March 7th)

In eternity, those who know the Lord will be eternally grateful for each trial encountered on earth. All tests and trials are flawlessly conceived and executed by a benevolent Creator. Every struggle in life is tailor made with us in mind, perfectly crafted by the Master surgeon Himself, with no possibility of malpractice—no chance of difficulties not working for our good.

Challenge your inner man, moment by moment, to return to the One who loves you the most. Train your soul in the way that it should go and when you are older your soul will not depart from the path of life.

The psalmist captured the essence of soul therapy. "Return to your rest, O my soul, for the Lord has dealt bountifully with you." (Psalms 116:7) The Lord does not deal more bountifully with one person over another. Certain people are just more successful in seeing their perspective triumph over their circumstances.

1. **How do you regularly train your soul to keep focused on the Lord during challenging experiences?**

2. **Are you able to experience joy and choose to be thankful for each trial you encounter?**

DAY

75 Planned Happiness

PRINCIPLE: I'LL ONLY BE ABLE TO SEE GOD WORKING IN MY LIFE WHEN I CAN SEE MY LIFE FROM GOD'S PERSPECTIVE.

A man in his early 90s lost his wife of 60 years. Realizing he could no longer care for himself, he decided it was time to move into a nursing home. On the morning of his first day, he arrived at eight o'clock sharp, neatly dressed and clean-shaven, with his hair meticulously in place. Legally blind, he sat for many hours in the lobby patiently waiting for his appointment.

When he was finally told where his room was, he smiled sweetly and began to maneuver his walker toward the elevator. While en route, the attendant escorting the elderly gentleman provided a verbal description of his tiny room. After hearing a brief assessment of the room's contents, the new tenant enthusiastically replied, "I love it."

Surprised at his response, the employee said, "Mr. Brown, you haven't even seen the room; just wait." Without missing a beat, the man replied, "That doesn't have anything to do with it. Happiness is something you decide on ahead of time. Whether I like my room or not doesn't depend on how the furniture is arranged…it's how I arrange my mind. I already decided to love it. It's a decision I make every morning when I wake up. I have a choice; I can spend the day in bed recounting the difficulty I have with the parts of my body that no longer work, or get out of bed and be thankful for the ones that do. Each day is a gift, and as long as my eyes open I'll focus on the new day and all the happy memories I've stored away, just for this time in my life."

What a tremendous outlook! Too many people spend their lives questioning if God really is concerned about their happiness. It all depends upon how we view happiness. If we define it as "a self-centered quest for personal fulfillment," then, it is true, that would not be God's objective for our lives. But, if we define happiness as the World English Dictionary does, then happiness is more than just a mere possibility, it is God's will for our lives.

The World English Dictionary's defines happy as:

1. feeling or showing pleasure, contentment, or joy;
2. causing or characterized by pleasure, contentment, or joy;
3. feeling satisfied that something is right or has been done right;
4. resulting in something pleasant or welcome.

The elderly man in the story had it right—happiness is not having what you want, it's wanting what you have. Thus, happiness is available to everyone—it's just a new perspective away. Nothing about the above definition requires selfish ambition or addiction to circumstances in order to fulfill happiness.

As Paul challenged us to be "exceedingly joyful in all…tribulation," (2Corinthians 7:4) so too we can rise above life's natural malaise and experience the supernatural presence of God in every situation. His grace is more than sufficient, if we allow His strength to rise above our weakness. (2Corinthians 12:9)

1 **What do you think of when you read the phrase, "happiness is not having what you want; it's wanting what you have?"**

2 **What are you looking forward to about today, and what God has planned for you?**

DAY 76

What Does "Better" Look Like?

PRINCIPLE: GOD HAS NEVER PREPARED ANYTHING FOR ME THAT WILL NOT WORK FOR MY GOOD.

In the end, how we respond to life is far more important then what happens to us. Oswald Sanders described it in a slightly different way, "Maturity is moving from a thin skin and a hard heart to a thick skin and a soft heart." That part of each of us that wishes things would get better is NOT our friend. Actually, that is our enemy. I have no idea what "better" looks like. That is why God has no intentions of fulfilling my expectations, but every intention of fulfilling His expectations through me.

I don't know what's best for me—never have, never will. I don't even know enough to have a strong personal preference. Spending my life wishing things would work out is an enormous waste of my time. The smartest thing I can do when it comes to how I would like things to work out is to remain neutral: no bias, fully flexible, and yielding to the will of the Father. God's been God for a long time; He's really good at it.

I need the same amount of faith to welcome the life God gives me, as I needed when I first embraced the God who saved me. We know we are trusting God when we stop wishing our lives would change. Love the life you have and joyfully receive every meal placed before you. My wife's pragmatic father would say to all four of his children seated around the dinner table when they would begin to complain about what was put before them, "Eat it! Your mother doesn't make anything that's not good." In life, God has never prepared anything for us that will not work for our good, no matter how it tastes.

1. **Have you ever reflected upon the importance of your responses in life?**

2. **Looking back over some past struggles, how do you think you would have responded differently if you chose to be neutral; no bias, fully flexible, and yielded to God's will?**

DAY

77 Storm Chasers

PRINCIPLE: THERE ARE NO ACCIDENTAL STORMS. EMBRACE EACH ONE.

Mountain Mike Shreve, a dear friend of our family, earned his nickname because he is one of the most knowledgeable men alive about the Sierra Nevada mountain range. Mike has lived his whole life in South Lake Tahoe and seen more snowstorms than he can remember. Located at 6,500 feet above sea level, Lake Tahoe provides some of the best skiing on Earth.

One Christmas, as we were visiting, he told me, "Heavy winters bring more bountiful summers." The comment sparked a revelation. We all appreciate spring flowers and summer fruit, but it's the dying in the fall and the storms of winter that bring the most bountiful harvests. Our failure to fully appreciate the storms of life merely demonstrates how shortsighted we really are. Interestingly, the opposite is also true; an over-dependence upon temporary satisfaction invariably leads to future disappointment. Bless the storms in your life, and stop chasing fleeting pleasures.

Mike also shared with me, "Every storm feels the same coming in; whether it brings two inches of snow or two feet." We never know which storm will bring the most challenge or the most benefit to our lives. Therefore, embrace storms as they come; there are no accidental storms. An omniscient God, who always has our best interest in mind, handcrafts every one.

But, don't lose sight if this fact as well. God has no desire to give you peace from the storms of life. His plan is to give you peace in the storm. Peace that comes when the storm stops is temporary. Learning to have peace during the storms of life is far better. This brings eternal blessings. We were created to meet Jesus in the middle of our storms. Frankly, few of us have time for Him outside of them.

1. **What helps you find peace in the storms of your life?**
2. **What benefits have you realized from storms?**

DAY

78 Drive Into The Wind

PRINCIPLE: THE PLAN OF GOD I CANNOT SEE IS GREATER THAN THE CIRCUMSTANCES I CAN.

A pastor friend of mine used to live in the Yukon Territory, one of the northernmost provinces of Canada. One winter day he went hunting on snowmobiles with a couple of natives.

Hours into their journey a violent storm came upon them. After a long period of fighting the snow, their lead guide gestured for the three of them to stop and talk. With howling winds and piercing snow buffeting them, they huddled together. The guide confessed,

"I think we're lost. I've grown up here my whole life, and I've never seen this rise in the terrain before." At those words the pastor's heart sank. Their guide was renowned. For him to be lost in a blinding snowstorm was terrifying and unexpected. After a few moments of reflection, the pastor sheepishly said, "We need to pray." Bowing their heads in desperation, they asked the Lord for His mercy and guidance.

Following an emotional prayer, one of them spoke up, "I believe we've been going in the wrong direction. Because of the intensity of the storm, we've been going with the wind.

What we need to do now is drive directly into the wind and snow." For a few moments after this unorthodox declaration they remained silent. Everywhere they looked was unfamiliar. In the middle of the whiteout, all they could hear was the sound of the howling wind and their pounding hearts. Each came to the jarring realization that either this radical recommendation was a Word of Knowledge, or it would lead them to certain death, going farther and farther away from safety until they would run out of gas.

After another desperate prayer, they decided to receive the counsel and headed off full throttle into the utter unknown. Though the wind and snow continued to batter them, they steadfastly drove directly into the storm. An hour or so passed when, finally, the guide stopped, knelt down and brushed away the snow from beneath them. He could see from the color beneath their feet that they were on a frozen body of water. He then told his companions, "Since we are on water, I believe I know where we are." He proceeded to lead them safely home.

What had saved their lives? In addition to the marvelous grace of God, they had been willing to do what hurt the most: face their fears and drive directly into the unknown. We only change when our willingness to accept God-allowed pain exceeds our fears. At times in our lives, we will all suffer a sharp painful disillusionment before we fully surrender. Even Jesus had to endure a painful crucifixion before He could say, "It is finished!" As we keep our eyes on the prize, we will eventually see all of the pressure and pain pale in comparison to the glory that will be revealed in us. (Romans 8:18)

My prayer is that the Lord will help each of us to see Him working in every moment of our lives. That He will lead us to trust that, the plan we cannot see is greater than the circumstances we can.

1. **What fears have you faced and terrifying circumstances have you confronted?**
2. **How has God changed you within these experiences?**

DAY

79 Giving All

PRINCIPLE: THE ONLY APPROPRIATE RESPONSE TO LIFE IS JOY.

Dr. Bob Pierce, founder of World Vision, a Christian relief organization, tells of an extraordinary event he witnessed with his own eyes. During the Korean War in the early 1950s, tens of thousands of refugees fleeing from the Red Chinese army attacking the north poured into South Korea. Under siege, in the middle of a freezing winter, the embattled city had lost all electric power. Churches opened their doors, having all night prayer meetings.

At four o'clock one morning, a dark, unbearably cold church was filled with multitudes of refugees. Women who had watched their homes burn and their husbands tortured to death sat in the frigid building holding their children close. Most were dressed in nothing but thin, padded cotton. The worship that night was filled with tears. In the midst of this traumatic scene, the pastor of the church decided to take an offering for the hundreds of refugees still coming into the city.

With great passion he entreated, "Something must be done to help those who are coming to us. What does this congregation have to give?" Those shivering in the crowded pews had lost their homes, businesses, and savings, and were themselves in desperate need. The pastor continued, "...and so we will give an offering of clothes." It seemed an unthinkable request; insensitive to the obvious needs of the people surrounding him.

Yet the pastor's appeal brought an extraordinary response. An elderly, emaciated man came forward, removed his vest, and solemnly laid it on the communion table. A young mother took the sweater off her baby and tucked the infant inside her own clothes. Soon, the table was piled high with clothes. Their lives were shattered and broken, but these nameless saints counted it all joy to literally give the clothes off their backs. If joy is how God responds to life, and if He is truly living in us, then joy must be how we respond to life as well.

1. **Have you ever experienced joy while in a very challenging situation?**

2. **What do you think caused you to be joyful?**

DAY 80 Unthinkable Joy

PRINCIPLE: GOD GIVES US EACH THE LIFE HE KNOWS WE NEED.

Can you ever imagine finding pleasure in your pain?

Paul the Apostle did. He endorsed this seemingly irrational line of thinking when he wrote, "I am exceedingly joyful in all our tribulation [Greek—pressure, affliction, anguish, burdens, persecution, trouble]." (2Corinthians 7:4) Is it possible to be grieved and joyful simultaneously? Absolutely! You might be brokenhearted someone has died, yet joyful he or she is in Heaven. You might be saddened your job is ending, but joyfully confident God has something better.

Faith is the miraculous ingredient that activates true joy in each of our lives. Whereas happiness sometimes waits to see what is going to happen, joy blissfully opens its arms to every moment, choosing in advance to see life from God's point of view.

The Bible gives us the perfect response to the calamities of life: "Weeping may endure for a night, but joy comes in the morning." (Psalms 30:5b) Yet it is possible for us to resist the joy that God desires to bring to us. Joy only comes in the morning, if we choose to let joy come in the morning. We can opt to let fear or worry come in the morning, or perhaps even depression and suicide. If we so desire, we can invite discouragement for breakfast, take hopelessness out to lunch, and join despair for a candlelight dinner. It's our call. I have spent enough time with each of these pathetic emotions, now I limit my life experiences to seeing joy in my circumstances. (1Peter 1:8) It is my choice how I choose to see the life God has given me.

Joy has to be invited into our lives and, once invited, must not be taken for granted. Just as Jesus focused on, "...the joy that was set before Him endured the cross..." (Hebrews 12:2b) we must concentrate on the joy set before each of us as we endure the hardships in life. Jesus took pleasure in His pain, and embraced the purpose behind His suffering. May God open our eyes to see that glorious purpose in our life as well.

When we spend our lives dwelling on yesterday, we shouldn't be surprised if tomorrow never comes. Instead of embracing what is happening in our lives, many of us feel empty about what is not happening. There's a better option: the next time you are going through hell, don't stop. We have a fanciful expectation of what we think we need, and when it doesn't take place we are disappointed. As God gives each of us the life He knows we need, we must therefore learn to embrace life as it is, not as we wish it were.

At the end of the day, this is really the only good option we have. Embrace it.

1. **How do you invite the joy of the Lord into every situation?**
2. **In what ways are you able to experience pleasure in your pain and embrace God's purpose in your suffering?**

DAY 81 The Cure for the Shattered Life

PRINCIPLE: TRUE SATISFACTION ONLY COMES FROM SEEING YOUR LIFE FROM GOD'S PERSPECTIVE.

In 2Corinthians 12:10, Paul the Apostle writes, "Therefore I take pleasure in [think well of, approve, am pleased with] infirmities, in reproaches [insults, hurts] in needs, in persecutions, in distresses [calamities, anguish] for Christ's sake. For when I am weak, then I am strong."

Did he really mean pleasure? Was Paul exaggerating when he said he thought well of, approved of, and was pleased with his insults and hurts? Or had his perspective been so radically transformed he actually found pleasure in being persecuted and insulted? It seems evident from scripture that Paul found the God of comfort in an extraordinary way in the midst of the distresses and calamities assaulting his soul.

So, what's the cure for a shattered life? Once again, it's the three-letter word: joy. I would personally define joy as "a deep sense of inner elation and satisfaction that comes from seeing your life from God's perspective, and responding properly to the challenges and suffering of life."

James, the brother of Jesus, taught the importance of responding well to suffering when he wrote, "My brethren, count it all joy [cheerfulness, calm delight, gladness] when you fall into various trials [adversities, temptations] knowing that the testing of your faith produces patience [cheerful or hopeful endurance]. But let patience have its perfect work, that you may be perfect and complete, lacking nothing." (James 1:2–4)

Who wouldn't want to be "perfect, complete, and lack nothing?" Yet, things coming up roses will not make this happen; we must allow situations to, at times, come up thorns.

1. **Have you ever chose to give God the control within a very distressing situation and experienced His comfort?**

DAY 82

Dead Men Have No Preferences

PRINCIPLE: THE ONLY COMFORT THAT LASTS ON EARTH IS THAT WHICH ORIGINATES IN HEAVEN.

Mike Bickle writes, "Satisfied people sin less. Much of the sin in the body of Christ is a wrong response to pain, fear and the need for comfort. Sin is a false comfort that people use as a prop to get them through seasons of pain. Many people get into sin because they feel beaten up and abandoned by God and men. Even though they are not truly abandoned, they feel that way. So they reach out for immediate comfort in status, financial gain or wrong expressions of sexuality." (Mike Bickle, *The Pleasures of Loving God*, 55–56)

God provides a better alternative. "Therefore let those who suffer according to the will of God commit their souls to Him in doing good, as to a faithful Creator." (1Peter 4:19) We know we are walking in resurrection life when we are more concerned about Heaven than Earth, and more interested in trusting God than understanding life's most asked question, "Why is this happening to me?"

The Apostle Paul concludes, "If then you were raised with Christ, seek those things which are above, where Christ is, sitting at the right hand of God. Set your mind [affections] on things above, not on things on the Earth. For you died, and your life is hidden with Christ in God." (Colossians 3:1–2) Dead men have no preferences. They bask in total acceptance and complete resignation; as R.I.P. implies, they Rest In Peace. It is God's will for each of us to have no preferences, not just when our bodies die, but when we choose to die to our own will and yield to Him. Die today! You'll be glad you did.

1. **What are your typical responses when you feel abandoned?**
2. **What do you experience when you choose to die to self and seek only the Lord for satisfaction?**

DAY

83 Drowning

PRINCIPLE: AWKWARD MOMENTS CAN LEAVE ME CONFUSED AND ANGRY, OR FULLY SURRENDERED AND BLESSED. IT'S MY CHOICE.

What keeps us from fully embracing the setbacks of life? Why do our hearts flinch when tested? Is it because we fear the unknown, or because we fail to trust the God we should know? Are we drowning in worry and unbelief, unable to see the infinite wisdom and eternal value of the suffering that God has tailor-made for each of us? We must learn to drown gracefully. Yet this goes against our natural instinct to survive. But what good is survival if it means living less than God intended?

Sebastian Junger, in his best-selling book The Perfect Storm, which was later made into a successful movie, describes the sequence a person goes through while drowning. Interviews with individuals who had drowned, but were resuscitated, chronicle every dimension of their chilling experience.

When a person begins to drown, the first emotion they experience is disbelief. They can't believe this is really happening to them. It is quickly followed by a sense of desperation. Next, there is a feeling of awkwardness; no one drowns gracefully.

Drowning invariably comes at an inopportune moment. A person drowning may think, "I can't die; I have tickets to the big game next week." This is followed by an acute sense of embarrassment. In their imagination, they see people shaking their heads because their death was so senseless. They feel stupid, and may think, "This is my last, great act of stupidity." Finally, as shocking as it may sound, after about 90 seconds, while still conscious, the drowning person takes in an involuntary breath of water.

Though it is unnerving for us to imagine ourselves drowning in water, it is equally disconcerting to watch someone drown in the perilous waters of life. The water-related sequence described above has many similarities to the stages an emotionally despondent person goes through when they despair of life.

In our mangled world, there is no shortage of people who feel as if they are drowning due to addictions, or because of poor moral, relational, or even financial choices. Every day, people drown in hopelessness and despair. Embarrassed by how messed up their lives have become, they often feel stupid for blowing it so badly. Always awkward, emotional drowning never comes at a convenient time. It is the last experience people want to have. Yet, God yearns to teach us a better response. One that defies hopelessness, laughs at calamity, and leads to a fearless life of peace and tranquility.

Trust in the God of hope when you feel desperate. Believe in His faithful promises. Drown gracefully, accepting that true humility—always embarrassing and awkward, eventually yields the eternal fruit of a fully surrendered and blessed life.

Recently, after receiving some jolting news that could have been seen as sad and disappointing, the Holy Spirit quickly reminded me of my only responsibility. I was in charge of the Respond Well Department; He was in charge of everything else. The world says, "Be in control." The Word says "Give God control." (Ephesians 5:18, NLT) What a relief! What a joy!

1. **Have you ever felt like you were drowning in hopelessness and despair?**
2. **What do you think God wanted to show you though this experience?**

DAY

84 Polar Twins

PRINCIPLE: NOTHING CAN EVER HAPPEN TO ME TO MAKE ME PESSIMISTIC.

A father had twin boys who were polar opposites. One was an optimist, believing everything would turn out great. The other was a pessimist, convinced that things always ended poorly.

One day, the father decided to do an experiment and placed each of the young boys in separate rooms. He put the pessimist in a room packed with every imaginable fun toy. He left the optimist in a room with just a giant bag of horse manure.

An hour later, the dad returned to the pessimist's room only to find the boy had not even touched the toys and was sitting idly in a corner. Dumbfounded, the father asked his son why he wasn't playing. Shrugging his shoulders, the boy replied, "Well, if I start playing with them I'll probably get bored or hurt myself, so I figured why even start?" Stunned at the pessimistic son's response, the father left the room shaking his head in disbelief.

Entering the other son's room, the father was shocked to find the optimistic twin completely immersed in the giant bag of manure. He was literally swimming in it; thrashing around as if searching for a ten-carat diamond. The father asked, "What are you doing?" His son looked up and grinned, "There's just gotta be a pony in here somewhere!"

Long ago, I settled in my heart to live as an optimist. I want to live life enthusiastically, wading through disappointments and delights alike.

Paul the Apostle, also an optimist, once wrote, "Now thanks be to God who always leads us in triumph in Christ, and through us diffuses the fragrance of His knowledge in every place." (2Corinthians 2:14) May my heart be that place.

1. **What would your life look like if you viewed it through the optimistic eyes of God?**
2. **What promises of God do you cling to for a heavenly perspective?**

DAY 85

Overcome Grief With Joy!

PRINCIPLE: THE CHOICE OF BEING OVERCOME BY JOY OR DESPAIR IS MINE ALONE.

The emotions of life are many and complex. One moment we are being overcome, and the next we are overcoming. As the Psalmist once wrote in the depths of despair, "Have mercy on me, Lord, for I am in distress. My sight is blurred because of my tears. My body and soul are withering away. I am dying from grief; my years are shortened by sadness. Misery has drained my strength; I am wasting away from within." (Psalms 31:9–10, NLT)

How ironic that, just two verses prior, he had written, "I am overcome with joy because of your unfailing love, for you have seen my troubles, and you care about the anguish of my soul." (Psalms 31:7, NLT) It seems the choice of being overcome by joy or despair is ever before us. If there were nothing to overcome, as in the Garden of Eden prior to the Fall, then we would have no reason to fight for joy. Like ripened fruit, it would just fall from the trees of life.But such is not the case.

Choosing fruit from the Tree of Life or the Tree of the Knowledge of Good and Evil each day remains in our court. Though what happens in life may seem to be completely out of our control, how we view life is always our choice. I can choose to see my life from God's expansive, life-giving point of view, or be limited by the myopic narrowness of fear, unbelief and ignorance which can only lead to emotions of panic, despair and anger.

For many of us, this is how we face our challenges. We are unable or unwilling to defeat the emotional onslaught seeking to destroy our lives; or we can look up, past the distracting struggles that keep us stuck in the past, bound in the present, and lacking hope for our future. May we resign ourselves in advance that whatever comes our way, we are choosing to remain "...steadfast, immovable, always abounding in the work of the Lord, knowing that your labor is not in vain in the Lord." (1Corinthians 15:58)

1 **Do you ever find yourself overcome one moment and overcoming the next?**

DAY

86 No Limitations

PRINCIPLE: TRIALS ARE MEANT TO BRING OUT THE BEST IN ME.

My wife and I once had lunch with a 24-year-old Christian lady in New Zealand named Debbie Ward. Aside from a strikingly joyful countenance, what made Debbie unique was the fact that that she was born with no lower half of her body: no feet, no legs, nothing below her waist. At the time we met Debbie she had been traveling around her nation speaking to groups of young people. She told us she began each talk by saying, “Don’t feel sorry for me! I love my life!”

She was so confident and wise in her convictions you couldn’t help but realize she indeed had been blessed with something special from God. Half a body had not limited her from having twice the character of most people. She loved her life; not just any life, but the one God gave her. In the same way Jesus gave Stephen a standing ovation in Heaven, (Acts 7:56) I believe this precious young lady will receive one too. Every time she confessed, “I love my life,” she became the tallest person in the room.

Trials are meant to bring out the best in us, not the worst. They throw the pass beyond our reach, but not beyond God’s intent and grace. He is the one who makes up the difference when we are weak and insufficient.

Oswald Chambers writes, “God does not give us overcoming life: He gives us life as we overcome.” (Oswald Chambers, *My Utmost For His Highest*, August 2nd) The discouragements of yesterday don’t disqualify you, the setbacks of today can’t sabotage you, and the failures of tomorrow won’t finish you. You were created to overcome.

1. **What is something you view as a setback that could actually be your moment to shine and chance to overcome?**

DAY 87 Great Paradoxes

PRINCIPLE: THE DOORWAY TO YOUR DESTINY IS THROUGH YOUR WEAKNESSES.

Most people miss one of the great paradoxes of life; mistakenly believing the doorway to their successes will be through their strengths. Not so! Our strengths are far more dangerous than our weaknesses, providing the easiest access to failure. It is our weakness that holds the key to unlock the grace of God. The Apostle Peter once wrote, "God resists the proud, but gives grace to the humble." (1Peter 5:5b) If pride is intrinsically resistible, then humility must be, by its very nature, irresistible. Humility is learning to fully embrace and delight in our weakness. It is that captivating quality of Jesus that releases the irresistible grace of God.

People's desires are not God's desires. They'll do anything to change the way they look—to change the shell—when God wants to transform the pearl. Cosmetic surgery will never make someone whole. Wholeness must be internal. In this age of genetic engineering, stem cell research, and designer children, we continue to substitute the Creator's flawless intent for our flawed perceptions.

Dream God's vision for your life, not a temporary one. It is pointless to complain about your job; instead, begin crying out to God for a new heart. We don't need a new life; we need to appreciate the one God has given us. The problem is, most people don't appreciate what they have. More often than not, we would gladly give up our own lives for the life of another. But in doing so we fail to realize we would be exchanging the life we have been given, that has been especially designed for us, for the life specifically designed for another. This is one of the key ways God uses celebrities: they show the world you can have everything in the physical world and still be unfulfilled. Embrace the life God has given you, not the life you think you should have.

Like Lucifer of old, who attempted to re-create the Universe in his own likeness saying, "I will ascend…I will be like the Most High…" (Isaiah 14:14) we have lost almost complete sight of what we have been given. Our inner longing to become Designer-Creators has evolved, in essence, out of godless self-promotion; attempting to birth children fashioned in our own image, even in the likeness of the shallow qualities that impress us but bore Heaven.

I remember reading about an elderly American woman who died of starvation alone in her apartment because she didn't have any money. Yet when the police examined her belongings, they found over $100,000 in cash buried inside the mattress she died on. The woman had stashed it away and then forgot about it. Our heavenly Father has buried amazing gifts deep inside each of us, yet how many of us have tragically lost sight of them?

Do we know what the God who shows no partiality (Acts 10:34) has equally dispensed to each of us? Do we love the life He has given us, or are we obsessed with what we don't have? The perfect promise in 2Peter 1:3 should be a pledge written on our hearts: "His divine power has given to us all things that pertain to life and godliness." Every challenge in life is designed to reveal our weakness and God's strength and to make us realize not just how desperately we need Him, but how absolutely sufficient His grace is in each of our lives. God has given us everything we need to love the life He has given us. Batteries are included!

1 What is something you consider weakness that, when surrendered to God, could be your greatest strength?

DAY 88

Response is Everything

PRINCIPLE: HOW I RESPOND TO EVENTS IN MY LIFE IS INFINITELY MORE IMPORTANT THAN WHAT HAS HAPPENED TO ME.

No aspect of our lives has ever been an oversight to God. "My frame was not hidden from You, when I was made in secret..." (Psalms 139:15) God has never made one mistake concerning our fragile lives. "...I am fearfully and wonderfully made...and that my soul knows very well." (Psalms 139:14) There has never been a recall of even one human being; all of us have been given infinite potential by a gracious God.

If we refuse to accept God's plan for our lives, we consign ourselves to a brave new world of perpetual unfulfillment. Waiting for a better life is like staring at your dinner, hoping to improve its taste. God's will is that we would come to the place where we love the life He has given us, instead of wishing for what does not exist and would not satisfy us even if it did. There is no faster way to get to where your heart really wants to be than through the will of God. Accepting and embracing the will of God is the Express Train to Fulfillment.

In life there are no shortcuts, only detours. Even if we momentarily transition into being pleased by life's circumstances, it will be short-lived. May we each accept the obvious: God is trying to change us, not change the world around us. In life, if we cannot appreciate what we have, we will never be pleased with what is ahead. If we cannot grow where we are, we will never bear fruit elsewhere.

Even those born with catastrophic physical deformities can be a catalyst for compassion, generosity and joy. Traumatic difficulties are not a roadblock to personal fulfillment. Seen from God's perspective, they can even become the doorway to a transformed life.

The primary reason people do not love the life God has given them is because they do not know and trust God. When we don't trust God, inevitably, we begin to play God ourselves. Judas thought he knew better than God the Son, as did King Saul, King Solomon, and most of the kings of Israel and Judah. Don't spend a lifetime envying others, when God is the only Person worthy of our worship.

Our misunderstanding of life should never tempt us into thinking God has lost His underlying sense of purpose for us. "Trust in the Lord with all your heart; do not depend on your own understanding." (Proverbs 3:5, NLT) The more I know me, the less I trust me; the more I know God, the more I trust Him. "It is better to trust in the Lord than to put confidence in man." (Psalms 118:8) That's when the joy comes. Only by completely trusting God can we become joyful. "But let all those rejoice who put their trust in You; let them ever shout for joy, because You defend them; let those also who love Your name be joyful in You." (Psalms 5:11) Jesus went one step further when He challenged each of us to the core. "Simply put, if you're not willing to take what is dearest to you, whether plans or people, and kiss it goodbye, you can't be My disciple." (Luke 14:33, The Message)

Kiss goodbye—what you can't keep! Kiss hello—what you can't lose!

1 **Reflect on Psalm 139 and being "fearfully and wonderfully made." List characteristics you appreciate about how God created you.**

2 **How do you depend on your understanding (sight) when you should be trusting in God (faith)?**

DAY 89

Calling All Fruit Inspectors

PRINCIPLE: WITHOUT A DRAMATIC CHANGE OF HEART, YOU CANNOT CLAIM TO BE "BORN AGAIN."

I know I am a fully surrendered Christian when my desires have changed into God's desires. If we claim to be a Christian and have not had a dramatic change of heart, we must accept the obvious: we need to be born again. Jesus said, "...a tree is known by its fruit." (Matthew 12:33) If we have been born again in the past, but our lives demonstrate little fruit, the ball is still in our court. Apparently, we must be born again—again.

According to Christian pollster George Barna, more and more people are confessing they are born again but fewer are living differently. Born again Christians are defined by Barna as people who said they have made a personal commitment to Jesus Christ and it is still important in their life today. They also indicated they believe that when they die they will go to Heaven, because they had confessed their sins and had accepted Jesus Christ as their Savior. Respondents were not asked to describe themselves as born again.

In his report on the state of Christianity in America Barna writes, "The worst thing would be for millions of people to accept Christ as their Savior, and then live the remainder of their life as if nothing had changed other than their eternal destiny. The challenge to faith communities, at this point, is to help people realize that you cannot be a follower of Christ by taking the free gift of salvation and then continuing to pursue the same life trajectory as before making that decision. Embracing Christ as your Savior is not the end of the story. It's the very beginning point of a transformed life that centers on constant worship of God, serving other people, investing personal resources in the values of God, deepening their relationship with God every day, and creating families that place God at the center of their shared experience."

When we receive God's Spirit, only then do we begin to see with God's eyes, and to feel with His heart. Until Jesus is Lord of our lives, all we will ever be able to become is religious—going through the motions of performing for God, but not knowing Him. We miss what life is all about. We miss having a deep, personal relationship with our Creator. "…the Lord spoke to Moses face to face, as a man speaks to his friend." (Joshua 33:11)

Jesus Christ's warning 2,000 years ago remains as potent as ever, "Not everyone who says to Me, 'Lord, Lord,' shall enter the kingdom of Heaven, but he who does the will of My Father in Heaven. Many will say to Me in that day, 'Lord, Lord, have we not prophesied in Your name, cast out demons in Your name, and done many wonders in Your name?' And then I will declare to them, 'I never knew you; depart from Me, you who practice lawlessness!'" (Matthew 7:21–23)

Knowing God is not an option, it is a necessity. If we are truly born again, our desire to draw close to God will grow in allowing Him to take His rightful place as the Lord of our lives. God has done everything He can to invite us into intimacy with Him. "Draw me away! We will run after you. The king has brought me into his chambers. We will be glad and rejoice in you…" (Song 1:4a) True relationship leads to intimacy with God, which in turn always leads to becoming more like His perfect Son, Jesus.

1 How do you live differently than before you became a Christian?

DAY

90 Terrible God

PRINCIPLE: THE MORE I LIVE, THE MORE I REALIZE THERE'S NO CRISIS I CAN FIX.

I would be a lousy God. I know this is true based on how I treat my friends when they are in trouble. I tend to want to bail them out of every crisis they encounter. Being God, I would spoil the whole planet. Not only do I not know what is best for me, I rarely know what is best for others.

In the movie *Bruce Almighty*, the title character is frustrated by how God is running his life. Bruce's adamant complaint leads to a sovereign test. God allows him to become God for a season and grants Bruce the ability to decide how to answer the prayers of an entire planet. Completely overwhelmed by the multiplied millions of requests pouring in, Bruce finally says, "Yes!" to everyone's prayers, no matter how selfish or shortsighted they may be. Only then does he realize that what he thought would help actually hurts—badly. Chaos ensues as every self-centered motive in the hearts of men is revealed.

The more I live, the more I realize there is no crisis I can fix. I will always need God. Though it is a natural human desire to meet someone else's need, the complexity of doing that is beyond my comprehension. God is infinitely more interested in fixing us than in fixing our problems. As a matter of fact, He is often the author of our problems. We're saying, "God, stop the problem!" He's saying, "Stop the whining and begin to understand what I am allowing."

When Jesus faced the greatest trials of His life, He didn't try and manipulate His Father in Heaven to lighten His load. Instead, Christ's pain only further revealed His true purpose in life. "Now My soul is troubled, and what shall I say? 'Father, save Me from this hour?' But for this purpose I came to this hour." (John 12:27)

We were born for trouble, created for a fight. It is only through trouble that our soul is formed, shaped, and molded into the image of an untroubled God. I love the overstated expressions "don't give me any good news, it only weakens me" and "if you are not living on the edge, you are taking up too much room."

Remove your troubles and you eliminate your purpose in life: to be conformed to the image of Jesus Christ. "For whom He foreknew, He also predestined to be conformed to the image of His Son." (Romans 8:29) Defining your purpose in life reduces frustration. Being created in the image and likeness of God (Genesis 1:26) was the beginning of your purpose. Finishing that work is now your destiny; it is where God is taking us. Your purpose is part of the reason why God is taking you there. Anything that keeps you from fulfilling God's ultimate purpose—being conformed to His image—must be disregarded and treated as a distraction. Tragically, most people live and die distracted.

As I look back over my life, my consistent appeals for God to make my life easier have not fallen on deaf ears due to indifference. The all-knowing, all-caring God has merely dismissed my fleeting appeals as narrow-minded, showing a lack of foresight and long-term planning. He has refused to bow to my ignorance, but has instead held fast to His wisdom. He knows the easy life would destroy my potential; therefore, He makes my life purposefully difficult.

Only by pressing the olive is the oil poured out; only by crushing the flower is the true fragrance released. Only as Paul was "pressed out of measure... insomuch that we despaired even of life" (2Corinthians 1:8, KJV) did the "sweet-smelling aroma, an acceptable sacrifice, well pleasing to God" (Philippians 4:18) come forth from his life.

1. **Reflect on a time when taking control made the situation worse.**

2. **How can you better acknowledge God as the author and perfecter of your faith? (Hebrews 12:2)**

DAY 91

I Love My Life

PRINCIPLE: IF I DO NOT LOVE THE LIFE GOD HAS GIVEN ME, I HAVE SOMEWHERE LOST TOUCH WITH THE GOD WHO SAVED ME.

I am training my soul embrace every second of my God-intended life. All days are equal. There is no best day in Heaven. Since before time began, a perfect God has flawlessly crafted every molecule, moment, and memory.

The Father has heard and answered the prayers of Jesus. "Your kingdom come. Your will be done on earth as it is in Heaven." (Matthew 6:10) God loves and favors each of us equally. He exercises His justice with absolute equity.

In John 12:25, Jesus challenges our shallow understanding of life. "He who loves his life [Greek—is attached to his life] will lose it, and he who hates his life in this world [Greek—loves his life less] will keep it for eternal life." If we are attached to our dream for our life, it will slip through our fingers. If, on the other hand, we embrace God's plan, whether we ever fully understand it or not, we will begin to live the pleasures of eternal life right now.

In this world, everyone experiences a measure of pleasure; everyone wins something! The devil is happy to give us the pleasures of Connecticut and Vermont Avenues, as long as he retains the pleasures of Boardwalk and Park Place. If you have ever played the board game MONOPOLY®, you know Connecticut Avenue and Vermont Avenue are virtually worthless. By obtaining these properties you have won nothing of real value. Similarly, counterfeit intimacy—which I call religion—is a shallow substitute for a personal relationship with a God who is madly in love with us. You have peace, but not lasting peace. It is joy, just not real joy. It is pleasure, without eternity.

"Religion is the Opium of the People." Karl Marx was right—but for the wrong reasons. Religion does drug people into a fog of lifeless rituals. But Marx never understood the distinction between religion and relationship. If he had pushed beyond the meaningless ceremony and encountered the person of Jesus Christ, he would have found something far more dynamic and life changing than communism will ever be.

Religion has little to offer the world except a system of conscience-soothing routines. But the world doesn't need cosmetic surgery; it needs a heart transplant. Only the power of Jesus Christ can perform that operation. Transformation must begin inside. A relationship with God Himself changes the heart first, and the rest follows naturally.

Real pleasure comes from real relationship, and you will never experience real pleasure until you get to know the only true God there is: the Lord Jesus Christ. Don't wait until you get to Heaven to experience the pleasures of knowing Him. You can enjoy His presence and His pleasure today in worship, in prayer, by washing your soul with God's Word, and by learning to be relationally connected with His family here on earth.

1 Are you growing in your relationship with Jesus, or merely stuck in religious traditions?

DAY 92

Stop Blaming God For Your Life

PRINCIPLE: IF YOU ARE RARELY CONTENT, THEN YOUR DISCONTENTMENT IS ULTIMATELY WITH GOD.

Something is terribly wrong when we wish we had a different life, when we don't look forward to getting up in the morning, when we think our best days are behind us, and that past mistakes have disqualified us from having a great future. If we are rarely or never content, then we are not in love with the life God has intended for us. It is not that each of us grew up experiencing only bad things. What many of us experienced was the absence of good things. Before it is too late, you need to begin to live the wonderful life God purposefully designed for you.

Even if our external life changed, we would not necessarily respond differently to life. Initially we might, but in the end we would all revert back to what we really believe. Our belief about life will always surpass our experience of life. We don't need to see more miracles; we need to respond properly to the ones surrounding us every day.

Jesus told the story of a rich man who died and was sent to hell. While there, he saw father Abraham in the distance and begged him to send someone to his five brothers to warn them of a similar fate. "Abraham said to him, 'They have Moses and the prophets; let them hear them.' And he [the rich man in hell] said, 'No, father Abraham; but if one goes to them from the dead, they will repent.' But he [Abraham] said to him, 'If they do not hear Moses and the prophets, neither will they be persuaded though one rise from the dead.' " (Luke 16:29–31)

If His contemporaries refused to believe the miracles of Jesus, why would anyone choose to believe our miracles? Such is the human condition. Unless someone experiences a dramatic inner transformation, his inner un-wholeness will taint his view of life. God has already done enough around me. Now I need to let Him complete His work in me.

1. **What miracles have you overlooked?**

DAY 93 The Purpose of Prayer

PRINCIPLE: HOPE'S SHELF LIFE IS ONLY FOR TODAY. TOMORROW IS PROMISED TO NO ONE.

I am not waiting for God to answer my prayers. The purpose of prayer is not to get answers, but to get to know God! I am not waiting for God to heal my body. Every external miracle will eventually leave me dissatisfied if it does not turn my attention back to God. This is a great seduction. Only one out of the ten lepers Jesus healed came back to thank Him. (Luke 17:17–18) Each external desire will immediately be followed by another request: "If this or that would just happen, then I can be fulfilled." I used to be obsessed with what I did not have; I battled depression over what was not happening in my life. I will never go back to that mindset again. I was wasting both my time and God's.

I once met a Christian man who had been the director of a psychiatric hospital for 25 years. I asked him what had surprised him most about people who are mentally ill. He said, "The fact that every patient I ever met was completely and utterly consumed with Self. It was Self in the morning, Self at noon, and Self at night." Focusing on Self is not the solution, it is at the very heart of the problem.

Oswald Chambers writes in *My Utmost For His Highest*, "Anything that has even a hint of dejection spiritually is always wrong. If I am depressed or burdened, I am to blame, not God or anyone else. Dejection stems from one of two sources—I have either satisfied a lust or I have not had it satisfied. In either case, dejection is the result."

Don't look to God to coddle you. Let Him comfort you.

Don't ask Him to answer your prayers. Ask Him to teach you to pray.

Don't live waiting for tomorrow to begin. Live hoping today will never end.

1 **List out people you want to pray for consistently and pray for them.**

DAY

94 It's Party Time

PRINCIPLE: JESUS DOESN'T WANT TO SHUT DOWN YOUR PARTY. HE WANTS TO INVITE YOU TO HIS.

When will we stop blaming God for our lives, and begin to bless Him for the magnificent, daily opportunities He's given each of us. When Jesus truly becomes our Lord, life becomes lovely. Every moment, every breath, becomes part of life's great adventure. As each thought is reigned in, each bows before a faultless God. (Philippians 4:8)

Now is the time to surrender our hearts to Jesus as Lord! Now is the time to remove every excuse for not loving the life He's given us!

The psalmist wrote, "All my springs are in You." (Psalm 87:7) The fresh water of life we are each thirsting for can only be found flowing from the throne of God. (Revelation 22:1) The contaminated streams of this world will never satisfy. Jesus said, "...the Kingdom of God is within you." (Luke 17:21) The kingdom of God is within me, if I will but look. Either I have the kingdom of God in me or I do not have it at all.

Jesus doesn't want to shut down my party. He wants to invite me to His. He has promised each of us, "If you believe in Me, come and drink! For the Scriptures declare that rivers of living water will flow out from within." (John 7:38, NLT) Even in the final verses of God's Word, He calls us to receive His abundant life, "The Spirit and the bride say, 'Come.' Let each one who hears them say, 'Come.' Let the thirsty ones come—anyone who wants to. Let them come and drink the water of life without charge." (Revelation 22:17, NLT)

Only Jesus can quench the thirst He created in us.

1 What excuses keep you from loving the life God has given you?

DAY 95 The African King

PRINCIPLE: GOD HAS AN UNLIMITED, PROTECTIVE WARRANTY THAT COVERS US IN ALL CIRCUMSTANCES, AT ALL TIMES.

There once was a king in Africa. He had a close friend who looked at life from a positive perspective. Whatever was transpiring, his friend would comment, "This is good!"

One day while the two friends were out hunting, the king gave his friend the responsibility of preparing and loading the guns. Yet somehow the friend made a mistake, for when the king fired a gun his thumb was blown off.

Immediately the friend made his characteristic response, "This is good!" The king was furious. He shouted, "No, this is not good," and immediately sent his friend to jail.

A year passed.

One day the king, while on another hunting expedition, went into a particularly dangerous region and was captured by a tribe of cannibals. The cannibals took him to their village, bound him to a spit, and prepared to make a fire beneath him. Yet just as they were beginning to light the wood, one of the cannibals noticed the king's missing thumb. A highly superstitious tribe, the cannibals refused to eat someone who was not completely whole. Instead of killing him, they untied the king and sent him away unharmed.

When the king returned home, he remembered how he had lost his thumb, and was saddened as he thought about the friend he had imprisoned.

Filled with remorse, the king went straight to the jail and told his friend what had happened with the cannibals, confessing to him, "You were right, it was good that my thumb was blown off. I am so sorry for putting you in jail for such a long time; it was a bad thing for me to do."

"No!" The friend once again responded. "This is good!" Startled, the king asked, "What do you mean, this is good? How could it be good that I sent you to jail for a year?"

The friend replied, "If you had not put me in jail, I would have been with you when you were captured by the cannibals, and they would have certainly killed and eaten me."

The friend's response to life demonstrates a marvelous principle. The same principle is found in Romans 8:28 when God promises every believer in Jesus Christ, "And we know all things work together for good to those who love God, to those who are the called according to His purpose."

Let's break this marvelous promise down:

"And we know"—not speculate or presume, but know with absolute certainty

"All things"—not some or even most situations

"Work together for good"—our benefit

"To those who love God"—more than anyone or anything else

"To those who are the called according to His purpose"—not pursuing their own desires or ambitions, but pursuing God's

To sum up this Biblical equation, "all things work for the good" for people with who meet two qualifications: 1. they love God, and, 2. they are called according to His purpose.

If you presently qualify for this wonderful promise from God, then rejoice and be diligent to train your soul to continuously trust in this warranty for life!

If, on the other hand, you do not qualify for God's full coverage plan, there is still time to change your mind. "This is good!"

1. **Do you have any doubt that ALL THINGS work together for GOOD? If so, why?**

2. **Do you love God above all else? If not, what idols need to be destroyed?**

DAY

96 Eternal Time Travelers

PRINCIPLE: UNTIL YOU EMBRACE A PERSPECTIVE THAT TRANSCENDS YOUR LIFE ON EARTH, YOU'LL BE OVERWHELMED BY THE DAILY GRIND.

When we completely love and are committed to the Lord, we're given the oppor-tunity of fully embracing the reality that there is no bad news in God. Yet we will only see this if we train our soul to believe from a broader perspective than the daily grind. We must embrace a perspective that even transcends our lifetime here on Earth. We must have eternity in our hearts (Ecclesiastes 3:11) in order to accurately assess if our lives have truly worked for our good.

The Book of Hebrews offers a glimpse into the mindset of heroes of the faith who refused to let their past or present rob their future. Many godly men and women have left the planet having not seen all they hoped for. Yet in spite of this, these fathers and mothers of the faith were fully persuaded that their hopes and dreams would one day be fulfilled.

"These all died in faith, not having received the promises, but having seen them afar off were assured of them, embraced them and confessed that they were strangers and pilgrims on the earth. For those who say such things declare plainly that they seek a homeland...But now they desire a better, that is, a heavenly country. Therefore God is not ashamed to be called their God, for He has prepared a city for them." (Hebrews 11:13–14, 16)

You don't need to receive the promise before you believe. You don't need your prayers answered before you trust. You don't need to be fully healed before you seek to heal others. You are complete in Him. (Colossians 2:10) And when you see Him face to face, you will be like Him. (1Corinthians 13:12) Till then, "be steadfast, immovable, always abounding in the work of the Lord, knowing that your labor is not in vain in the Lord." (1Corinthians 15:58b)

1 **Is there something you believe needs to take place in your life before God can use you? What are you waiting for?**

DAY

97 Embracing Life

PRINCIPLE: SUCCESS IS LEARNING TO EAT THE MEALS GOD PLACES BEFORE YOU WITH A GRATEFUL HEART.

There's only one way to follow God: by faith. Unless we walk by faith, one day we will find we are not following Him at all. It takes great faith to believe the promises of God more than our circumstances, but we each have been given enough faith to do so. Romans 12:3 assures us, "God has dealt to each one a measure of faith." Jesus adds, "...if you have faith as a mustard seed, you will say to this mountain, 'Move from here to there,' and it will move; and nothing will be impossible for you." (Matthew 17:20b)

What mountains of pain and discouragement are you facing? What mass of misery threatens to bankrupt your entire investment in God? John Osteen, the father of Joel Osteen, would often challenge his Houston, Texas congregation: "Stop telling God how big your mountains are, and start telling your mountains how big your God is."

I need the same amount of faith to embrace the life God gives me, as I needed to embrace the God who saved me. It takes no faith to say, "God has not given me a life worth loving." On the other hand, it takes great faith to believe the truth, "God can only give me a life worth loving." Like any good father, God gets far more glory out of us living fulfilled lives than unfulfilled; and unlike our earthly fathers, He is completely capable of making our fulfillment a reality. The primary problem we have is that we often fail to see our lives from God's point of view.

As we wade through a smorgasbord of life's circumstances, we must resist the temptation of rejoicing in only the opportunities that suit our fancy. The truly successful pilgrims of earth learned to eat the meals placed before them with grateful hearts.

1 **If faith comes by hearing, and hearing from the Word of God, have you nourished your faith well?**

DAY 98 The Goal of Life

PRINCIPLE: LEARN TO REST SO COMPLETELY IN GOD'S PERFECTION THAT YOU ARE NOT OVERWHELMED BY YOUR OWN LACK.

In order to change the visible realm, we must learn to see into the invisible. The main goal in life is to see the eternal realities and not just the temporary distractions of earth. Our time here is a dress rehearsal for eternity. Every aspect of our life is a test. God will not give us new revelations of Himself until we are obedient to the revelations He has already given us. Therefore, if we mistakenly take our eyes off of the revelations we have already been given, eventually all we will see are our problems.

The more we get to know the perfect, completely captivating God, the more transformed our lives become. Truly living for Jesus should always bring greater satisfaction, not less. If we are not satisfied with the life He has given us, it is because we have our eyes focused on self and not on God. Only when we are fully satisfied with who He is will we at last be satisfied with the life He has purposed for us.

The closer we get to God, the more our understanding of perfection increases. As we grow in our knowledge of Him, we should feel increasingly less and less perfect—but it should not discourage us.

As we grow more attached to His perfection, we will be less stumbled by our own imperfection. The goal in life is not to measure up to God. That would be futile! Instead, the goal is to learn to rest so completely in His perfection that we are not overwhelmed by our own lack.

Most of the time, no one can hurt me more than I can hurt myself and no one can bless me more than God. I have found God's Word to be true. "The blessing of the LORD makes a person rich, and he adds no sorrow with it." (Proverbs 10:22)

1 **Do you struggle feeling you don't measure up to God, or do you believe you are secure in His heart toward you?**

DAY 99

Looking Good In Bad Lighting

PRINCIPLE: GOD SEES MY IMPERFECTIONS CLEARLY, AND YET HE LOVES ME DEARLY.

We will always look our best in bad lighting. Add some alcohol to the mix and even unattractive people look pretty good. On the other hand, if we want to really see how we look we need to turn up the lights. Doctors' offices intentionally do not have bar room lighting and good doctors are never intoxicated when they examine patients. They want an accurate assessment of how their patients look; only more light can provide this.

There are occasions, however, when we are not necessarily looking for the most accurate representation of ourselves. Whenever our family goes to a professional photographer to get our picture taken, we don't care if the finished product is an exact representation of us. We'll take all of the help we can get in order to look our best.

Though a family portrait would be one of the few occasions we allow our self-image to be altered, it is impossible to imagine a doctor telling a patient, "I took a look at your x-ray and saw some significant abnormalities, but don't worry about it—I touched up the x-ray. Now it looks great!"

None of us would find comfort in someone attempting to alter reality in a life-threatening dimension. We all want our x-rays to be an accurate portrayal of what is really going on because, in this case, unreality would destroy us. Don't mess with my x-rays!

So how does a perfect God relate to His imperfect creation without lowering His standard of perfection? John, the beloved Apostle, affirms the purity of God when he writes "God is light and in Him is no darkness at all." (1John 1:5) Just as the closer we get to good lighting the worse we look, the closer we get to God the worse we look. That doesn't sound very exciting. Yet as we draw nearer to God we can see Him more clearly and we can see He is smiling because of each of us. (James 4:8) What an incredible dichotomy! I'm looking worse and His smile is getting bigger. My value to Him has nothing to do with how I see myself, and is only based on how He sees me. He sees me clearly and yet loves me dearly.

The satisfaction we are looking for will not come from God answering our prayers, it comes from learning to trust Him regardless of His answer. Therefore, the best response we can ever give to God is to smile back at Him.

God completes each of us and that completion took place long before we were created. Jesus prayed, "Father, I desire that they also whom You gave Me may be with Me where I am, that they may behold My glory which You have given Me; for You loved Me before the foundation of the world." (John 17:24)

Just as the Father loved Jesus before the foundation of the world, He also loved us. (John 15:9) We are as loved by the Father as Jesus is, and that sacred romance began long before we even existed.

"Behold what manner of love the Father has bestowed on us, that we of all people should be called children of God!" (1John 3:1)

1 What evidence do you have to believe God smiles at the thought of you?

DAY 100

Life's Unthinkables

PRINCIPLE: LIFE IS ALL ABOUT LEARNING TO THRIVE IN UNTHINKABLE SITUATIONS.

An Australian missionary I once met spent years ministering to a South Pacific tribe without seeing any converts. One day, a member of the tribe accidentally electrocuted the missionary's nine-year-old son. The clan had a custom that when someone was killed, the victim's relatives had the right to take revenge on the person responsible for the death. They expected the missionary to kill the one who had killed his son. But instead of exacting retribution, the missionary forgave his son's murderer. His response sent a shockwave through the tribe. They could not believe the missionary would not seek revenge.

Eventually, because of his selfless attitude, the entire tribe came to know Jesus. The missionary family had experienced an incomprehensible loss. But because of their willingness to receive the grace of God, he and his wife were able to offer unthinkable forgiveness.

Unthinkably challenging experiences are on the horizon for each of us. They will catch us totally by surprise and can shake us to our core. Most of the time they are events we thought would never happen—things that a loving God would never allow. When they occur we may begin to question what we have never questioned before. How we respond to these unthinkable events in life will determine whether we become bitter or better.

Life is filled with the unthinkable. We don't mind the good unthinkables of life, like receiving an inheritance from a wealthy uncle you never met. But it's the seemingly bad unthinkables: the sudden death of a loved one, divorce, chronic pain, or a terminal illness that rock our world. Yet, if we respond properly to the unthinkables, they can bring us to a whole new place of faith in our walk with God.

1 Have the unthinkables in your life made you bitter or better?

DAY 101 Bible Unthinkables

PRINCIPLE: BIBLE HEROES LEARNED TO THRIVE IN UNTHINKABLE SITUATIONS.

There were many unthinkables recorded in the Bible: Lucifer rebelled against God; Adam and Eve attempted to deceive God; Cain killed his brother Abel; Jacob's sons sold their brother Joseph into slavery; 20 years later Joseph reveals himself to his brothers as the second-in-command in Egypt; Judas betrays Jesus; and Peter denies Jesus three times.

Since the beginning of the world, unthinkables have happened. Yet, the Bible repeatedly shows that when someone goes through unthinkable trials with a proper attitude, God will grant him or her the grace to accept, and even thrive, in the situation.

Joseph, after being thrown into prison for fleeing from evil and clinging to what was good, maintained a good attitude toward both God and man. "…because the Lord was with him; and whatever he [Joseph] did, the Lord made it prosper." (Genesis 39:23)

Job experienced an unthinkable loss when all of his ten children perished. That same day, all of his possessions were stolen and painful boils broke out over his body. Yet, he refused to curse God. Because he responded properly, God blessed the end of Job's life more than his beginning, giving him ten additional children and twice as many possessions. (Job 42:12) For years, King Saul chased David, and was intent on killing him. Yet, the promise of God to David remained steadfast, "…in everything [David] did he had great success, because the Lord was with him." (1Samuel 18:14)

Even Jesus experienced the greatest tests of His life when all of His disciples abandoned Him; when His mother watched Him die a gruesome death; and—the greatest unthinkable of all—when He lost fellowship with His Father by becoming sin for the whole world. Yet, here too, He conquered sin and death, and became "…the firstborn among many brethren." (Romans 8:29)

1 What was the key ingredient that made Bible characters flourish even in unthinkable situations?

DAY 102

Success is Where You Finish

PRINCIPLE: THE TRUE TEST IN LIFE IS SEEING "THERE'S NO BAD NEWS IN GOD."

None of choose where we start, but we where we finish is a different story. On November 6, 1986, Bob W. Ireland finished the New York City Marathon in 19,413th place. It was the slowest marathon time in history. It might not have been a noteworthy event, except for the fact that Bob was the first person to run a marathon with his arms, instead of his legs. A 40-year-old California native, Bob had his legs blown off in Vietnam in 1969. Though it took him four days, two hours, 48 minutes, 17 seconds, when asked why he ran the race, Bob, a born again Christian, said, "Success is not based on where you start, it's where you finish."

One day driving on a highway in South Lake Tahoe, California I saw Bob Ireland running on his hands on the side of road. The thing that made this image particularly astounding was the fact that he was running down a steep grade, in snow flurries. I was stunned and prayed for this courageous man.

In the final book of the Bible, the Book of Revelation, the highest honor is given to one type of person: the Overcomer. Jesus Christ, the greatest Overcomer of all time, said, "He who overcomes, I will make him a pillar in the temple of My God, and he shall go out no more. I will write on him the name of My God and…My new name." (Revelation 3:12)

The true test of the overcoming life is being able to see that, in God, there really is no bad news. The main issue is not our placement in the marathon of life, but rather what we've had to overcome to place at all. May we each finish well.

1. **Do you see your life finishing well? Why?**
2. **What value do you put on faithfulness? What value does God put on it?**

DAY 103 Spiritual Whiplash

PRINCIPLE: "WHAT WE CALL THE PROCESS, GOD CALLS THE END." OSWALD CHAMBERS

Many years ago I was encouraged to read the classic daily devotional by Oswald Chambers *My Utmost For His Highest*. Chambers had been a missionary to Egypt in the early part of the 20th century. Though he died in his mid-40s of appendicitis, he left a rich legacy of revelations for generations to come. Presidents of nations have read his devotional and leaned on the profound insights it provides.

Chambers' teachings were so weighty that at times I was shocked by his conclusions. I remember thinking there must have been typos in the book, because some of what I read seemed so outlandish. In 1990, around the time I had received the rejection for my youth tour proposal, I read the following quote "We must never put our dreams of success as God's purpose for us; His purpose may be exactly the opposite. We have an idea that God is leading us to a particular end, a desired goal; He is not. The question of getting to a particular end is a mere incident. What we call the process, God calls the end." (Oswald Chambers, *My Utmost For His Highest*, July 28th)

What a concept! This quote dramatically changed the way I processed the will of God. Before receiving this revelation I had always believed God's goal for my life was for me to do great things for Him; it was the end result that really mattered. I hardly chewed my food; rarely smelled the flowers, and consequently never felt that what I had accomplished on any given day was good enough to meet the expectations of a perfect God. I was a man on a mission, with no time to waste. Constantly busy about my Father's business, but never believing I was fully capable of doing it. I figured I would rest when I arrived at where I was going. The problem was; I was so fickle I never arrived.

As I processed Chambers' quote I realized God's primary goal was to transform my inner man to look like Him. He was far less concerned about the events in my life; His primary focus was my heart. I had been driven by an inner need for acceptance and self-worth when God, having already completely accepted me, wanted to draw me by His Spirit.

If we refuse to embrace the process—every aspect of what we are going through—we will miss the entire point of life.

1 Do you spend you life dreaming of the end or embracing the process?

2 How can you better enjoy your life-in-progress?

DAY

104 Abiding

PRINCIPLE: ABIDE AND LIVE, OR RUSH AND WITHER.

All of us want our life to count.

There are secrets to this level of success.

In the Gospel of John, Jesus calls us to slow down and commune with Him. "I am the true vine, and My Father is the vinedresser. Every branch in Me that does not bear fruit He takes away; and every branch that bears fruit He prunes, that it may bear more fruit. Abide in Me, and I in you. As the branch cannot bare fruit of itself, unless it abides in the vine, neither can you, unless you abide in Me. I am the vine, you are the branches. He who abides in Me, and I in him, bears much fruit; for without Me you can do nothing." (John 15:1–2, 4–5)

We live in an age where few know how to abide. Our culture trains us to spend our days rushing through life, preoccupied with outward accomplishment and having lost sight of the greater work God wants to do in each of us.

In John 15:1–2, Jesus was saying, in essence, "Stay plugged into Me and I'll empower your life; stay on the operating table, and you'll bear much fruit. But if you get off, all you'll have is a gaping hole and flying intestines."

Jesus emphasized this point in John 15:6–7, "If anyone does not abide in Me, he is cast out as a branch and is withered; and they gather them and throw them into the fire, and they are burned. If you abide in Me, and My words abide in you, you will ask what you desire, and it shall be done for you."

Abiding is clearly not optional in the Christian life. We are each given a graphic choice—abide and live, or wither and be thrown into the fire. The second part of verse seven is only true if we are doing the first part. Lots of people claim the right to "ask whatever you desire" but are not complying with "if you abide in Me and My words abide in you." Asking whatever we desire is not a magic wand. It is contingent upon abiding in Jesus and allowing His words to abide [dwell, endure, be present, remain] in us.

Life is all about healthy growth that leads to bearing fruit; the only way for that to happen is to dwell in the Author of life. "By this My Father is glorified, that you bear much fruit; so you will be My disciples." (John 15:8) Which makes parents happier: when their children succeed or when they fail? In the same way parents delight in their children and want them to succeed in life, God the Father is most glorified in us when we are most fruitful in Him. Though God's definitions of success and failure are different than ours, a continual, conscious dependence upon Jesus will always lead to healthy growth.

May we each bear fruit that remains forever.

1. **When you focus on God's heart and your relationship with Him, are you at peace?**

2. **What do you need to believe about God in order to be at peace when you are with HIm?**

DAY

105 Deafening Silence

PRINCIPLE: IN THE SILENCE OF YOUR LIFE, LEARN TO HEAR GOD SPEAK.

Generally speaking, we hear the voice of God clearest in winter. During the more fragrant and fruitful seasons of our lives we are frankly, too busy, too distracted. In winter, all we have is time. We've been rained-out, snowed under, or frozen solid. At last God has our attention. If we spend our time wishing winter was over, we will miss the reason God created it in the first place—time to rest, listen, and be restored.

Here again, Oswald Chambers provides some extraordinary insights. "When God gets us alone by affliction, heartbreak, or temptation; by disappointment, sickness, or by a broken friendship; when He gets us absolutely alone, and we are dumbfounded, and cannot ask one question…then He begins to expound." (Oswald Chambers, *My Utmost For His Highest*, January 13th)

If you are questioning God about the season you are in, you are not fully embracing it. When God is in complete control of our lives we feel no need to ask Him questions. Questions indicate we have an agenda that we think we know what should be happening in our lives. In short, questions indicate a lack of trust. Babies have no questions, only acceptance and complete trust resting in their parent's arms. God wants to get us to a place where we are speechless, helpless and fully dependent upon Him. That kind of faith pleases Him the most. Jesus insisted, "Assuredly, I say to you, whoever does not receive the kingdom of God as a little child will by no means enter it." (Luke 18:17) An unbelieving planet resists loudly, while the Kingdom of Faith persists quietly.

Richard Wurmbrand, the Romanian pastor who spent 14 years in prison for his faith once wrote, "The one thing you Americans are most afraid of is silence." How true.

Let us learn to listen. As God spoke the world into existence (Genesis 1:1–3), He can speak life to every dimension in our lives as well.

1. **Take a moment to just listen to God. What do you hear Him saying?**

DAY 106 Fasting Feasts

PRINCIPLE: DON'T GORGE YOURSELF ON THE CRUMBS OF EARTH; HUNGER FOR THE TRUE FEASTS OF HEAVEN.

When I fast, and by that I mean give up some pleasure for a season whether it be food, entertainment, sports, or desserts. I eliminate the distractions in my life so that I may fully focus on what is truly eternal. I quiet my soul to hear the voice of God. I don't fast because I think I'm hyper-spiritual; I fast because I know I'm not. Fasting doesn't bring out the best in me; it exposes the worst. Spiritual toxins bloat and constipate my relationship with God. It is only when I allow the Spirit and the Word to wash over my soul that I am cleansed from the distractions of life.

Life tends to make us callused. Fasting softens and humbles us. It forces us to see ourselves as we really are—frail and needy. Paul the Apostle admitted he needed to fast often. (2Corinthians 11:27, 2Corinthians 6:5)

In Matthew 4, Jesus was led by the Holy Spirit to go into the wilderness to be tempted by Satan. He fasted 40 days and nights. Then "the tempter came to Him, he said, 'If You are the Son of God, command that these stones become bread.' But Jesus answered and said, 'It is written, "Man shall not live by bread alone, but by every word that proceeds from the mouth of God.' " (Matthew 4:3–4) Jesus needed the humility of fasting to activate the raw power of the Word of God. Masses of humanity gorge themselves on the crumbs of Earth; not realizing their true hunger is for the feasts of Heaven.

The earth is filled with people "whose end is destruction, whose god is their belly, and whose glory is in their shame—who set their mind on earthly things." (Philippians 3:19) Many years ago, when safes had rotary combination locks, thieves would use their fingers as hypersensitive listening devices. The most astute safecrackers would file the calluses off their fingertips in order to become more sensitive to the slightest gyrations of the lock. In fasting, we file away the hardness of life, in order to hear the still, small voice of our Creator. When we fast, we are encased in the process of getting to know God. Distractions are starved out; true feasting begins.

Jesus told His startled disciples, "I have food to eat of which you do not know," (John 4:32) and "My food is to do the will of Him who sent Me, and to finish His work." (John 4:34)

Each of us have been created and called to some great work for God. Fasting will help us hear His will and receive His power. May we each make this vital spiritual discipline a regular part of our lives.

1. **Have you experienced the value of fasting in your own life?**

2. **What areas of your life would you fast in order to be drawn closer to God?**

DAY 107

We Were Once Darkness

PRINCIPLE: ONE OF THE GREAT MIRACLES IN LIFE IS BEING ABLE TO LOVE LIGHT MORE THAN DARKNESS.

Though many of us have at times been afraid of the dark, darkness was the very first season the creation experienced. "In the beginning God created Heaven and earth. Now the earth was formless and empty, darkness was over the surface of the deep, and the Spirit of God was hovering over the waters." (Genesis 1:1–2, NIV)

In the beginning of all things there was darkness; but darkness, by its very nature, is insatiable. It is the gnawing repetition of darkness that makes us crave the light. No one ever ended their life wishing they had given themselves over to greater darkness. The opposite is true. When I gave my life to Jesus, I was so sick of the darkness I wanted to end my life.

I'm still sick of darkness.

Solomon illustrated this principle when he wrote, "Honey seems tasteless to a person who is full, but even bitter food tastes sweet to the hungry." (Proverbs 27:7, NLT) I can remember many nights during my life when I couldn't wait for the night to be over and morning to come. Every day there are people who frantically long for their night of desperation to be over and a day of hope to dawn at last.

Each day is likewise a microcosm of the four seasons. It begins in darkness (12:01 AM), often the coldest part of the day. Metaphorically speaking, we launch our day in winter. Gradually, the morning warms up and we enter a type of springtime. During the heat of the day, we experience a mini-summer. As the sun sets and it starts to cool off, we enter fall.

All of our lives start out in darkness: both natural and spiritual. Yet though we all have the option of moving into the light, most people on the planet are still in darkness. "If we say that we have fellowship with Him, and walk in darkness, we lie and do not practice the truth." (1John 1:6) "This is the crisis we're in: God-light streamed into the world, but men and women everywhere ran for the darkness. They went for the darkness because they were not really interested in pleasing God." (John 3:19, The Message)

Men love darkness; yet God still loves men.

As John Newton, the author of the famous Christian hymn Amazing Grace wrote, "I once was blind, but now I see." If we have been born again, we are now called to walk in the light. "For you were once darkness, but now are you light in the Lord. Live as children of light." (Ephesians 5:8, NIV) One of the greatest miracles I have ever seen has taken place in my own heart. I, who once loved darkness, now love light. If there is a greater miracle than that, I have never seen it.

1. **Is there more light in your life than darkness?**
2. **What practical steps can you take to move closer to the light?**

DAY 108

The Best Season of Your Life

PRINCIPLE: IF THERE IS A BEST SEASON IN LIFE, IT SHOULD BE THE ONE YOU'RE IN.

If you don't know the season your life is in, you're going to have a really hard time.

If you are looking for fruit on your tree in the middle of winter, you are going to be disappointed. If you are trying to hold on to parts of your life in the fall, when emotional leaves are falling away, you will be very frustrated. It is a waste of time to pine for springtime in winter, lust for summer in spring, and long for fall in summer. The fruit of each season is designed to bring us closer to Jesus so he can bring healing to our lives. (Revelation 22:2)

When God wants spring to come in your life, it will happen. But we do ourselves a distinct disservice by refusing to embrace what is right in front of us. Spring flowers will come soon enough. In the meantime, don't miss what God is trying to show you today.

The Message Bible says it quite well. "Give your entire attention to what God is doing right now, and don't get worked up about what may or may not happen tomorrow. God will help you deal with whatever hard things come up when the time comes." (Matthew 6:34) I have wasted too many wonderful days, in magnificent places, with fascinating people, because I was unable to get my heart around what was happening, and instead longed for what was not. I will never get those days back, but I am committed to relearn what I missed then.

There is no best season in life. When I received Jesus as my Lord and Savior, it was a springtime experience. I was so high I thought I would never come down. Then came a seemingly endless summer when all kinds of fruit surfaced in my life. But when, in time, fall arrived and I lost the warm fuzzies, I got really discouraged.

Once-healthy leaves were falling off every dimension of my life. I desperately longed for spring and summer again, but things only seemed to get worse. Instead of being revitalized, I felt more and more dead. My heart was frozen in the winter of my discontent. I whined, squawked, and begged God to restore what once was. But He had no interest in playing reruns; He had brand-new dimensions of character He wanted to reveal in me. He was committed to conforming me to His own image: the God of ALL seasons. As a loving Father, He refused to yield to my naïve complaints. In the end, spring did return, but the cycle of life and death would be revisited over and over throughout my life.

Some people hate winter when everything they were attached to lies dead at their feet—but everyone goes through winter. Frankly, I believe our best season in life should be the one we are presently in. It really is a matter of perspective.

1 In what ways are you living the life God dreamed for you?

DAY 109 God For All Seasons

PRINCIPLE: IN WINTER, YOU WILL TEND TO THINK YOUR FUTURE IS DEAD.

Initially, as a young Christian, all I longed for were the springtime and summer experiences in God. Over time, however, I realized every season has its pitfalls. King David was seduced in the spring (2Samuel 11:1–2) and Adam and Eve had their great fall during the summer. (Genesis 3) I began to realize that during prolonged fall and winter seasons, God was able to do a much deeper work in me than He was through the flowers of spring and fruit of summer.

I learned to embrace the dying of fall, as once flourishing dimensions of my life seemed to wither and drop off. These desperate seasons provoked me to become more attached to God and less to what I thought I needed from Him. It was during my spiritual winters when my life appeared dead and frozen that God performed the deepest internal transformation within my soul and spirit. I would not trade the profound work God has done in me for life in an easier season.

The first disciples started out their spiritual walk in springtime. It seemed that following Jesus made everything better. Around the time Jesus raised Lazarus from the dead, Christ's ministry was peaking. "If He can raise people from the dead," His disciples thought, "He could liberate us from Rome." In the history of the world, the notion that Christ's goal was in some way tied to liberating his followers from Rome has to be one of the most serious under assessments of a person's potential ever recorded. They didn't realize until after He was dead that Christ's greater goal was to liberate them from something far more dangerous than the Roman Empire—themselves. The enemy within was a greater threat to their purpose and destiny than all of the oppression of Rome.

Soon after Jesus raised Lazarus from the dead, He told his disciples He was leaving. His disciples freaked out saying, "Lord, you don't understand. We're booked. We've got overflow crowds, the TV networks are lining up... you could run for Prime Minister!" Jesus shrugged. He knew that winter was coming, and the sell-out crowds were about to shrivel. After the crucifixion, the multitudes dwindled from multiplied thousands to everyone fleeing, from 500 people who personally saw the resurrected Jesus to 120 people in an upper room, praying once again for spring.

We must know in which season we are in order to receive the full benefit of God's perfect plan. "The stork knows the time of her migration, as do the turtledove, the swallow, and the crane. They all return at the proper time each year. But not my people! They do not know what the Lord requires of them." (Jeremiah 8:7, NLT)

Peter, not knowing the season he was in, made promises to Jesus he couldn't keep. "'Lord, why can I not follow You now? I will lay down my life for Your sake.' Jesus answered him, 'Will you lay down your life for My sake? Most assuredly, I say to you, the rooster shall not crow till you have denied Me three times.'" (John 13:37–38) How can I embrace a season if I insist on denying I am in it? Once again, I have to know where I am in order to get where I need to go.

Let Jesus prune you! Let Him trim off what is dead and stinking. Let Him remove what has no lasting value and will only weigh you down. Soon you will rebound from your winter, basking among the beautiful flowers and sweet fruit of a fully surrendered life, reflecting on how wonderful your winter was—no longer dreading fall and winter's return.

1 **Can you imagine embracing every season of your life equally?**

2 **How could 'winter' become your favorite season?**

DAY

110 Fruit Is Not Optional

PRINCIPLE: YOU WILL TEND TO RESIST GOD WHEN HE IS REMOVING SOMETHING DEAD FROM YOUR LIFE.

Jesus admonished, "I am the true vine, and My Father is the vinedresser. Every branch in Me that does not bear fruit He takes away; and every branch that bears fruit He prunes, that it may bear more fruit." (John 15:1–2) Every challenge God sends our way is designed to make us more fruitful. He removes areas in our lives we have been attached to, some of which are now dead. Though they may have previously been highly fruitful, they are now a hindrance to our future growth.

God is not enamored by how we look on Earth. As a wise Father, He is committed to firmly establishing our internal, long-term health. Therefore, He cuts away what we are attached to, even what appears to be healthy, in order to produce His destiny for our lives.

Pruning is not hacking; it is precision trimming. A significant pruning may not look attractive initially, "nevertheless, afterward it yields the peaceable fruit of righteousness to those who have been trained by it." (Hebrews 12:11b)

So, what is the value of God pruning in our lives?

1. Pruning exposes obscure and hidden areas in our life to air and light.

2. Pruning corrects and repairs damaged branches in our life that have died for unknown causes. Dead branches should be removed as soon as we see them. If they are diseased, pruning will keep the infection from spreading to healthy areas in our life.

3. Pruning encourages flowers and fruit to come forth. Flowers soon become fruit, allowing the seeds contained within the fruit to produce new life. Pruning brings forth a beauty that can only be revealed as we die to ourselves.

4. Pruning directs and controls future growth. When we trim off side branches, we encourage growth in the main trunk. So often in life we give our energy to dead branches that drain us and keep us from growing in other areas. If we wait too long to trim off dead branches there can be extensive injury to the

trunk. “Purge out the old leaven, that you may be a new lump.” (1Corinthians 5:7) These draining branches can include relationships, friendships, bondages, entertainment, or addictive behaviors.

5. Pruning is necessary after we have gone through a significant transplanting in our lives. The very nature of transplanting means roots will be severed. When we’re wounded, we are pruned so we can grow healthy.

6. Pruning rectifies bad judgment. At times, a planter will mistakenly place a tree in a spot that it will eventually outgrow.

7. Pruning is essential in order to lessen the damage a tree will experience during storms. What could have been corrected in its infancy became a life-threatening travesty.

8. When God is at work in our lives, He prunes! When it is large, He uses bulldozers. Sometimes it’s radical! But do not fear; in time, old fruit orchards are pulled up and new ones planted. All for the good! For a few short years you will not see the fruit you once did. But get ready, in God’s perfect time your harvest will be abundant.

1 What has been previously fruitful in your life that now may be a hindrance to your future growth?

2 What do you think God’s pruning will accomplish in you?

DAY 111 Obstacles Are Opportunities In Disguise

PRINCIPLE: EVERY IRRITATION IS AN INVITATION TO GO TO THE NEXT LEVEL.

Frustrations are veiled doorways to our destiny. Until we see our lives from God's point of view, we will never see the good that is possible because of these frustrations. If we obsess over the pain and displeasure inherently associated with the struggles of life, we will miss their entire point. Each of our lives are intentionally shrouded in secrecy; our true purpose disguised in a maze of problems. Complaining about the setbacks only distracts us from receiving the truth behind the mystery. The key to life is to not stop at the surface of a problem, but to dig deep enough to uncover the reason and value behind each trouble.

From this moment on, let your default attitude be "God, what marvelous thing are You trying to show me through the challenges I am presently facing?

Though Paul the Apostle was in prison and would eventually be beheaded, he still saw how God graciously used for good what Satan meant for evil. Refusing to see his circumstance in a negative light, Paul wrote, "Now I want you to know and continue to rest assured, brethren, that what [has happened] to me [this imprisonment] has actually only served to advance and give a renewed impetus to the [spreading of the] good news [the gospel]." (Philippians 1:12, Amplified)

In 1962, Victor and Mildred Goertzel published a revealing study of 413 famous and exceptionally gifted people, called Cradles of Eminence. The couple spent years attempting to understand what produced such greatness, what common thread might run through all of these extraordinary people's lives.

Surprisingly, the most outstanding fact was that virtually all of them, 392 out of 413, had to overcome very difficult obstacles in their lives in order to become who they were. It's a fact! Difficulties in our lives are the greatest shapers of our destiny.

1 **Who are the personal heroes that you esteem because of the obstacles they overcame?**

DAY 112

Perfectly Positioned for the Rest of Your Life

PRINCIPLE: IF GOD CAN'T PROTECT ME, I CAN'T BE PROTECTED.

Absolutely everything we have gone through in life has prepared us for the God-conceived opportunities and challenges ahead.

When my family and I lived in Los Angeles, our then 14-year-old daughters were invited to a slumber party with some of their friends. We were told to drop our girls off at 11:00PM, despite the fact that the party was in a very rough part of town. When my wife and I arrived at the dimly lit street, we immediately began to assess our surroundings.

As we looked down the empty street, we could faintly see four silhouettes fanned out across the road. They were spaced apart and walking toward us at a slow, menacing pace. Though the girls were anxious to see their friends, I told them to wait, lock their doors, and stay in the car.

The four figures came closer to our vehicle. They were clearly members of a gang. But instead of passing us by, one guy, the largest one of the group, walked to the rear of our car and stood facing us. He folded his arms stiffly together, staring us down.

We froze. For at least a full minute no one spoke or moved. Finally, feeling the need to do something, I decided to get out of the car to talk with him. I reached for the door and unlocked it, but when I tried to pull on the door's handle, nothing happened. Click. Click. Click. Still nothing. I tried to lock and unlock the door repeatedly, but it would not open. I could still see the young man standing behind our vehicle, and I knew he could hear my pathetic attempts to open it. In an awkward kind of way, it was embarrassing. I couldn't even open my own car door.

Finally, I watched him angrily unfold his arms and wave his hands at me in disgust. He turned and walked away, rejoining his friends. When they were out of sight, I had one of my daughters get out of the back seat and let me out. I walked the girls to the house and then my wife and I drove away.

Yet my door, which had worked flawlessly until that moment, still would not open. A few days later, I invited a mechanically-inclined friend over to my house, and we took the inside of the door off. What he showed me was startling. The inner workings of the door had not broken. As impossible as it may seem, the two connected parts just separated. We both agreed, in the natural it couldn't have happened; yet it did. Jesus said, "What is impossible from a human perspective is possible with God." (Luke 18:27, NLT)

In retrospect, I don't think the gang member wanted to chat or have a Bible study. I believe my decision to get out of the car was a bad idea and God protected my life. Most likely I (and perhaps even my family) would have been seriously harmed. My Father in Heaven had miraculously intervened. It is a vivid demonstration of how He watches over every aspect of our lives. "He will not let you stumble and fall; the One who watches over you will not sleep." (Psalms 121.3, NLT)

It was God's will to show Himself strong on my behalf. I was perfectly positioned to see the miraculous hand of God and I didn't even know it. We are each continually positioned for success. All that is needed is for our hearts to remain open and trusting, surrendered to the One greater than our meager little plans.

1. **Describe a time God intervened in your life to protect you.**
2. **Have you grown more confident in God's ability to protect you?**

DAY

113 Face Your Fears

PRINCIPLE: HOW SUCCESSFUL YOU ARE IN LIFE WILL DEPEND UPON WHEN AND HOW YOU COME OUT OF HIDING.

Every day people perish for lack of understanding, living so much less than God intended. (Job 36:12) I once read about a young girl who spent 87 days in a row eating her lunch in a bathroom stall at school because she felt so insecure and rejected.

I can relate. During my pre-adolescent years, while living in the strict, all-boys boarding school, we would take daily, mandatory showers in a large, open room. Much to my personal embarrassment, it was obvious to all that I was one of the last to develop body hair. I felt completely inadequate and worthless. With no one to talk with about the issue, I solved the problem by spending months hiding in a bathroom stall during evening shower time. In order to appear as if I had taken a shower, I would put water in my soap dish, and then sprinkle it over my head before exiting the stall.

On a few occasions, I remember the sick feeling of thinking I had been caught, though I never was. Even as I write this, some 45 years later, I still feel the excruciating humiliation of this youthful trial. If only my story were unfamiliar to the human condition. But mankind has been prone to hide since the Garden of Eden. (Genesis 3:10) Why do we hide from the God who loves us, and from the divinely orchestrated events designed for our maturing and growth? If we face our fears, they will dissolve. If we bow down to them, they become bondages, strongholds, and even generational curses.

Are you in any way hiding, either from God or people? In order to be healed, you must walk out into the light of God's love, forgiveness, comfort, and power. His love covers. His grace forgives; and God's Spirit comforts and empowers us to be fully healed.

1 **Are there hidden dimensions in your life you are not allowing God and others to touch?**

DAY 114 I Hope Someone Notices When I Die

PRINCIPLE: MAY YOUR BELIEF THAT YOUR BEST DAYS ARE AHEAD NOT DIMINISH YOUR EMBRACING EVERY ASPECT OF TODAY.

Three weeks before Christmas in 1993, a 43-year-old man in Berlin, Germany, died while watching TV. No one noticed he was gone. His rent continued to be paid automatically out of his bank account. Five years later, when his money had finally run out, his landlord entered his apartment to see what had happened. He found the man's remains in front of his TV. The TV Guide was opened on his lap to December 3, 1993, the presumed day of his death. Although the television set had long since burned out, the lights on his Christmas tree were still twinkling away. What a grim finale to a forgotten life.

I hope someone notices when I die. I hope that my presence will in some way be missed. I hope I live such a life of caring for others, that at my point of need someone cares for me. May we never give up on God or people. May our hearts and minds remain steadfastly open to see our lives as God intended. May we always believe that our best days are always ahead.

I know even when I feel overlooked by others that I am never invisible to God. Jesus has promised each of us that our Father in Heaven is aware of all our needs. "Are not two sparrows sold for a copper coin? And not one of them falls to the ground apart from your Father's will. But the very hairs of your head are all numbered. Do not fear therefore; you are of more value than many sparrows." (Matthew 10:29–31) We must continually remind ourselves how invaluable, even priceless, we are to our heavenly Father. Behind every challenging circumstance, there is a loving God whose victorious perspective is far greater than the trial we face.

1. **If you could ask God to remove an area of self-absorption in your life, what would it be?**

DAY 115

Who's Holding Your Rope?

PRINCIPLE: DON'T POSTPONE LIVING TODAY FOR A TOMORROW THAT MAY NEVER COME.

Many years ago, there was a fishing village next to a turbulent river. One day a boy fell into the river. A crowd quickly gathered. A rope was brought and the strongest swimmer in the village volunteered to rescue the boy. He tied one end of the rope around his waist, threw the other end to the crowd and jumped into the river.

The crowd watched him swim through the violent current to reach the terrified child. When he finally grabbed a hold of the boy, the crowd cheered and people began to yell, "Pull in the rope!" As the villagers looked at one another, someone shouted, "Who's holding the rope?" No one was holding the rope. In the excitement of watching the rescue, the crowd had let the end of the rope slip into the water. Powerless to help, all they could do was watch the boy and his would-be rescuer sink beneath the devouring waters and drown.

Who's holding the rope in your own life? Who's healing your past? Who's sustaining your present? Who's securing your future? Decide now. Tomorrow may be too late. Don't learn how to box when you are fighting for your life. Don't figure out how to fire your gun when the thief is coming through your bedroom window. Fight for your life now! Don't postpone living today for a tomorrow that may never come. Jesus challenged us, "Therefore do not worry about tomorrow, for tomorrow will worry about its own things. Sufficient for the day is its own trouble." (Matthew 6:34)

"Whatever happens, dear brothers and sisters, may the Lord give you joy. I never get tired of telling you this. I am doing this for your own good. I don't mean to say that I have already achieved these things or that I have already reached perfection! But I keep working toward that day when I will finally be all that Christ Jesus saved me for and wants me to be." (Philippians 3:1, 12, NLT)

1 **Is there anyone you are accountable to, if your life was in trouble?**

DAY 116

The Cure for Boredom

PRINCIPLE: IF YOU ARE BORED, IT'S NOT GOD'S FAULT.

Boredom is a result of being unable or unwilling to see life from God's perspective. The God who made galaxies isn't boring. If we say we are following God and yet lack the passion and purpose He intended, then we have somewhere along the way lost touch with who He really is. Consequently, without knowing who He is, we can never realize who we are

Marco Prado, a pastor at The Rock of Roseville, once challenged our church family, "How many adventure movies do we have to watch before we begin to live the adventure God has planned for us?"

Every second we spend wishing we were somewhere else, or perhaps even someone else, is a waste of time and a slap in the face of a God who has done everything possible for our well-being.

We must stop waiting to live and start living!

Perhaps, it is the will of God for certain things to change in your life. Even so, "Unless the Lord builds a house, the work of the builders is useless." (Psalms127:1, NLT)

Let God direct and build your life and you will never be bored again.

Let God have your heart and He will fill it with His love and character.

Our God-given opportunities are quickly slipping through our fingers. Unless we open our eyes, we will miss parts of life we will never see again. "Awake, O sleeper, rise up from the dead, and Christ will give you light." (Ephesians 5:14, NLT)

1 **Is your life an adventure or a sleeper?**
What can you do to be passionate everyday?

DAY

117 Effortless Faith

PRINCIPLE: CONTRARY TO MOST PEOPLE'S PERCEPTION, FAITH REQUIRES NO EFFORT WHATSOEVER.

Faith only requires surrender.

True faith is effortless; like ripened fruit, it falls into our hands with ease. Jesus promised, "For My yoke is easy and My burden is light." (Matthew 11:30) A partial faith in God is really distrusting Him. In the same way a hospital patient, about to be operated on, must fully submit to the will of the attending health professionals, completely trusting the judgments and decisions that are beyond his or her control, we must likewise trust God by fully submitting to His will for our lives.

God has not brought you this far to fail, but to finish well. Paul the Apostle was "confident of this very thing, that He who has begun a good work in you will complete it until the day of Jesus Christ." (Philippians 1:6) God will finish what He has started in us and we will be more than just pleased; we will be amazed! If we yield to His plan for us, God promises our lives will be "exceedingly abundantly above all that we ask or think, according to the power that works in us." (Ephesians 3:20)

We don't need God to do one more thing for us. What He has previously done and is presently doing is more than sufficient. He doesn't have to demonstrate even one more time His love and care for my life. He has done enough. If we can just remember, if we can keep spiritual amnesia from overtaking our shallow consciousness, then we are set for life. In our right minds, we will overflow with gratitude. With a proper view of the panorama of our lives, the only appropriate response to a loving God is "thank you" a million times over.

We should be increasingly grateful to a generous Creator who has flawlessly fashioned every dimension of our lives.

1 What is the biggest step of faith you've ever taken?

DAY 118

Adventures or Disasters?

PRINCIPLE: WHETHER MY LIFE IS AN ADVENTURE OR A DISASTER IS IN MY COURT.

Many of us have had experiences in which we came within a whisker of losing our lives. At times, our brush with death so terrified us it became a memory we would rather forget. Several years ago I traveled to Italy to visit my sister and her family. My nephew picked me up at the airport in Rome. From there, it was a four-hour drive to my sister's home in southern Italy. I was completely exhausted, and began to doze off as he navigated the rain-soaked roads.

As we exited the highway, on the final stage of the journey, he took a 90-degree turn much too fast. The streets were slick and there was nothing that could be done. As my nephew shouted, "We're going over!" I cried out, "Jesus, help us!" We catapulted over a 30-foot cliff, and began to tumble end-over-end. I had no idea how far down we would go or if we would survive. But, as God would have it, the car came to a sudden, jolting, stop, right side up.

The first thing I felt was the sensation of cool rain falling on my face through the car's smashed-out windows. I was still alive! You never realize how safe you are until your protection is suddenly and violently removed. Our belongings had been thrown from the car and lay all around us, yet we had been left seat-belted inside and miraculously unhurt. Aside from the fact that my nephew had just totaled his future father-in-law's new Alfa Romeo, no harm was done. Though our tumble down a mountainside ended well, it was terrifying.

On the other hand, on many occasions I have actually paid lots of money to be jostled around. Theme parks across the world are packed with eager participants who venture onto thrilling and seemingly dangerous rides. Instead of screaming in terror, we screech with delight as we precariously dangle hundreds of feet above the ground or miss colliding with certain death by mere inches.

The difference between these two experiences boils down to one simple word: trust. Because we trust that the theme park equipment has passed the necessary safety requirements, we relax and enjoy; as soon as the ride is over we often get back in line for one more turn.

But what if one day, as we were waiting in line, a person was thrown from the ride, with his mangled body landing at our feet? Would we decide to get on that ride anyway? No one would; we would be crazy to do so. Even if the ride supervisor attempted to explain that the accident was a fluke and that it could never happen again, no one would go on that ride. In fact, some people would begin to question the safety of every other ride in the park.

The day trip would be over, but the ramifications could last for years. If the accident was significantly horrific, we may never try a thrill ride again. We might not just be done for the day; we might be done for the rest of our lives.

A serious breech of trust changes all perceptions. We have each seen the kind of trauma a breach of trust can bring upon an unsuspecting life, in relationship breakdowns, sporting and transportation accidents, and tragedies of all kinds. What once was greeted with wide-eyed anticipation is now a haunting memory.

This type of jarring experience keeps many people from loving the life that remains. God is blamed, vows are made, curses are activated, fear comes in, and faith takes flight. Just as we all sin and fall short of God's best for our lives, we each also battle a deep, underlying sense of failure. Unforgiven sins, an unhealed past, and unknown tomorrows paralyze most people on the planet, leaving them unable or unwilling to experience the many blessings God intended.

We don't have to understand what is going on in order to feel better—we just have to trust. If an unwavering trust can be restored and our confidence re-established, we will return to the joy of the journey.

1 **Is your life a thrill ride or a cliff ride?**

2 **How can a change of perspective make your life all that God intended?**

DAY 119 Interpreting Struggles

PRINCIPLE: WRAP YOUR ARMS AROUND THE ONLY COMPLETELY TRUSTWORTHY PERSON IN EXISTENCE.

All of us have read about or known people who have revisited their greatest fears in order to conquer them. They refused to allow past hurts to permanently mar their experience of life. Many of the people we consider heroes today hold that place in our hearts because they refused to give up.

Today, we all face this very same challenge. The sinless Lamb once again yearns to take our trust relationship to new heights. Every doorway to our future is purposefully designed to be entered with child-like faith; with arms reaching high into the air, completely confident and captivated by the Faithful One.

He has never failed us and He never will.

Even when we fail, it is not a deal breaker. It is another opportunity for us to grasp the nail-scared hand of a gracious God who willingly gave His life for us so that fellowship could be restored and not broken. Even "if we are unfaithful, He remains faithful, for He cannot deny Himself."(2Timothy 2:13, NLT) He cannot deny what is in His heart. And that passion, as The Message paraphrase so clearly tells us, "God put the world square with Himself through the Messiah, giving the world a fresh start by offering forgiveness of sins. God has given us the task of telling everyone what He is doing." (2Corinthians 5:19)

We have misinterpreted our past struggles and blamed an innocent God. It is time to cast our fears aside, disregard past misunderstandings, and rejoice in the God who is. We must wrap our arms around the only completely trustworthy Person in existence. Who, whether we realize it or not, is the only One who has never failed us. We finally grasp what life is all about when at last we realize God has always been there for us and always will be. (Matthew 28:20)

1 Is there a specific event in your past that you need to stop blaming God about?

DAY 120

The 2nd Half Only Gets Better

PRINCIPLE: LIVE THE REST OF YOUR LIFE KNOWING GOD IS FOR YOU.

During the 1930 Rose Bowl football game between Michigan and USC, Michigan fumbled the ball. A USC player named Roy Rigel recovered it and, to the shock and horror of his teammates, Roy picked the ball up and began to run the wrong way. Not just for a few yards but, like a man possessed, Roy ran for 95 yards. It wasn't until just before he reached the wrong goal line that he was tackled by one of his own men. Michigan scored, which turned out to be the winning point.

At halftime, Roy sat by himself on the floor with a towel over his head and tears in his eyes, completely devastated. He had done the unthinkable! He had run the wrong way! At the end of halftime, his coach said he wanted the same men who played the first half to go out and start the second. Roy sat there as if he hadn't heard a word. Finally ,his coach looked directly at him and insisted, "Roy, didn't you hear what I said? The same men who played the first half are going to start the second!"

It is recorded that Roy Rigel went out and played one of the most fierce and aggressive halves of football in USC history. He just needed one thing: a second chance. All of us are looking for a second half, another shot; one more opportunity to make up for the mistakes of the first half. Today, receive God's second chance; receive the gracious prodding of the One who has never given up on you. He has already covered our mistakes in His precious blood and forgotten our sins.

It is now up to us to receive the free gift of His forgiving love, and return to the 2nd half of our lives with renewed assurance that God is for us. (Psalms 56:9)

1 **Do you believe your best days are ahead? Why or why not?**

DAY 121

Forget the Good Old Days

PRINCIPLE: YOU ARE CALLED TO BUILD WHAT HAS NEVER BEEN BUILT BEFORE.

"Remember the good old days?"

Whoever came up with that statement must have had a bad memory. Which would you prefer, the old man or the new man; the old covenant or the new covenant? There has always been a conflict between the old and the new. That's why Jesus said you can't put new wine in old wineskins or new patches on old clothes. (Matthew 9:16–17) He backed this up with His own example, giving those who had been swamped with old commandments one all-important new one: to love one another. (1John 4:7–8)

We were created particularly to like new things. God, Himself, is so interested in new things that He has promised to make us a new Heaven and a new Earth. The same God who got a kick out of creating the universe instilled in us a deep appreciation for that which is fresh, clean, and new. We like new clothes, new hairstyles, new homes, and new cars. No one goes shopping with the hope of buying a worn-out car or a moth-eaten, fifth-generation jacket.

I am not knocking what is old. Age often has majesty, elegance, and nostalgia. But without reservation, I am convinced that new is better. Life is always new. Would anyone want to give birth to an old baby?

Never! When a baby is born, it's brand-spanking new.

"Behold, I will do a new thing, now it shall spring forth; shall you not know it? I will even make a road in the wilderness, and rivers in the desert." (Isaiah 43:19) Aren't many Christians wandering through a wilderness and desert? That's not God's intent! "'For I know the plans I have for you,' says the Lord. 'They are plans for good and not for disaster, to give you a future and a hope.'" (Jeremiah 29:11) Perhaps you personally need a new job, a new house, a new body, a new perspective, a new vision, a new purpose, a new outlook on life, or a new relationship with God, His Word, and prayer. God alone has the spare parts for all of your needs.

Where are you? Do you find yourself settling for the mediocre, the predictable? Does the faith that once inflamed your imagination now taste like stale toast or soggy Cheerios? Have yesterday's failures dulled your hope for tomorrow? I'd rather have MONOPOLY® hotels on Mediterranean and Baltic, than be stuck with the mortgages on Boardwalk and Park Place! I'd rather be given a clean slate or a fresh start, than make one more feeble attempt at repairing the un-repairable.

We are called to build what has never been built before. Out of the ashes of the moral, social, economic, political, and spiritual demise of our society will emerge the Church Triumphant. That's why God is offering us a new beginning and why He's even provided the recipe: "Purge out the old leaven, that you may be a new lump." (1Corinthians 5:7) If we are willing to give up the old, God is eager to make our lives new. Give up your old, tired, troubled perspective. Trade it in for the mind of Christ. Jesus said, "The words that I speak to you are spirit, and they are life." (John 6:63)

Let the Word of God become the life for which your soul longs.

1 How do you envision a triumphant End Times church?

DAY 122

The God of New Beginnings

PRINCIPLE: LET THE FEARS OF YESTERDAY BE ECLIPSED BY THE FAITH OF TODAY AND THE HOPE OF TOMORROW.

Once a year at midnight, a strange ritual takes place. In homes, hotels, Elks Clubs, and pool halls, a shout goes up all over the world, "Happy New Year!" The Earth begins another long lap around the sun giving people 365 more days to live up to a new set of resolutions.

So what's the big deal? If no one told us that 12:00:01 AM on January 1st was such an enormous event, I doubt we'd notice any astronomical change. One year would simply fade into the next. Time would be an endless loop, punctuated only by the jumps we make from one waist size to the next.

Our New Year's enthusiasm is another indelible sign we are created in the image of a merciful God—the God of New Beginnings. Aren't you glad He isn't the God of Old Endings? Our Lord is unquestionably more concerned with tomorrow than He is with yesterday. That's why He has slated finite time for now and infinite time—the eternal tomorrow—for later. God describes what is taking place down here as a vapor, a moment. (1Corinthians 15:52) In Heaven, things are everlasting and never-ending. Everything up there is forever new: new bodies, new surroundings, even new names. Yet the joys of tomorrow must be accessed by faith today.

"Every desirable and beneficial gift comes out of Heaven. The gifts are rivers of light cascading down from the Father of Light. There is nothing deceitful in God, nothing two-faced, nothing fickle." (James 1:17, The Message)

Step into eternity. Let the fears of yesterday be eclipsed by the faith of today and the hope of tomorrow. A change of mind is all that is needed; surrendering to the loving will of a benevolent God. Your best days are ahead if you want them to be. That was God's plan from the beginning and His flawless will for your life. Now you have to decide if it is your will.

1 If you could get a new lease on life, what would you ask God to do?

NOTES